2021

Awesome Creatures

Edited By Debbie Killingworth

First published in Great Britain in 2021 by:

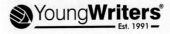

Young Writers
Remus House
Coltsfoot Drive
Peterborough
PE2 9BF
Telephone: 01733 890066
Website: www.youngwriters.co.uk

Printed and bound in the UK by BookPrintingUK
Website: www.bookprintinguk.com
YB0474C

★ FOREWORD ★

Welcome Reader!

Are you ready to discover weird and wonderful creatures that you'd never even dreamed of?

For Young Writers' latest competition we asked primary school pupils to create a Peculiar Pet of their own invention, and then write a poem about it! They rose to the challenge magnificently and the result is this fantastic collection full of creepy critters and amazing animals!

Here at Young Writers our aim is to encourage creativity in children and to inspire a love of the written word, so it's great to get such an amazing response, with some absolutely fantastic poems. Not only have these young authors created imaginative and inventive animals, they've also crafted wonderful poems to showcase their creations and their writing ability. These poems are brimming with inspiration. The slimiest slitherers, the creepiest crawlers and furriest friends are all brought to life in these pages – you can decide for yourself which ones you'd like as a pet!

I'd like to congratulate all the young authors in this anthology, I hope this inspires them to continue with their creative writing.

★ CONTENTS ★

Abington Vale Primary School, Northampton

Chrissie Chitura (8)	1
Caitlin Hughes (9)	2
Celesani Bhebe (9)	3
Orla Collis (9)	4
Kenzo Bain (9)	5
Maja Kusnierek (9)	6
Abraham Zahran (8)	7
Ben Hateley (9)	8
Lola Newman (8)	9
Myles Houghton (9)	10
Sophie Winston (8)	11
Phoebe Wingrove (9)	12
Iggy Thurlow (9)	13
Joseph Kanguni (8)	14
Siyona Patel (8)	15
Emily Bignell (9)	16
Heer Patel (8)	17
Maximilian Kufuor (9)	18
Lacey Tilley (8)	19
Isla Hallett (9)	20
Lex Tilley (8)	21
Oli Forbes (9)	22
Jack Brennan (8)	23
Noah Parker (8)	24
Andrew McGourty (9)	25

Banchory Primary School, Tullibody

Robbie Thomson (11)	26
Kyle Bryce (11)	27
Charlie Edwards (11)	28
Keira-Angel Hammond (11)	29

Katherine Bowie (12)	30

Erpingham CE Primary School, Erpingham

Saffron Howell (10)	31
Beth Catleugh (10)	32
Kris Chapman (11)	35
Lily-Beth Hollinger (10)	36
Tyler Fenton (9)	39
Esme Marling (10)	40
Kayden Wright (9)	42
Alaina Bray (10)	44
Cameron Carter-Lee (10)	46

Fort Hill Integrated Primary School, Lisburn

Chloe Adams (7)	47
Lucy Jelly (8)	48
Jackson Smith (8)	49
Ala Pieniak (9)	50
Sofia Smith (8)	51
Caleb McCready (9)	52
Chloe McCormick (9)	53
Lillie McLoughlin (8)	54
Katie Murray (8)	55
Matthew Simpson (9)	56
Imogen Champness-Curran (8)	57
Thomas Calinski (9)	58
Leina Johnston (8)	59
Callum Elder (8)	60
Alice Gray (7)	61
Charley Kirkpatrick (9)	62
Lily Dougherty (9)	63
Alex Korbik (8)	64

Oliver Fulton (8)	65	Poppy Porter (10)	112
Joel Tait (8)	66	Issy Bevan (10)	114
Taylor Gray (9)	67	Kayce Bridge (10)	115
Rosie-Anne McGrath (8)	68	Blake Burton (10)	116
Brody McFarland (9)	69	Daniel Critchley (10)	118
Sam Naga (8)	70	Georgia Ball (10)	119
Abigail Kennedy (8)	71	Abigail Sharp (10)	120
Abigail Heaney (9)	72	Mia-Rose Wilson (10)	121
Helena Parker (8)	73	Elena Thompson (10)	122
Ethan Edgar-McAleenon (8)	74	Alice Hosey (10)	123
Oscar McCutcheon (9)	75	Skye Peers (10)	124
Jack Meneary (8)	76		
Fabko Budo (9)	77		
Blake Reid (9)	78		

Milesmark Primary School, Rumblingwell

Jake Duncan (8)	79	Kaycie Comrie (11)	125
Georgia Friars (8)	80	Finlay Rees (11)	126
Corey Currie (9)	81	India Wilmshurst (11)	128
Connie Green (9)	82	Jessica Thomson (11)	129
Jack Porter (8)	83	Joseph McDermott (9)	130
Carter Greer (7)	84	Phoebe Ward (12)	131
Mason Duff-Dalzell (8)	85	Imogen Douglas (11)	132
Amy Graham (8)	86	Imogen Richmond (10)	133
Alex Stevenson (9)	87	Nieve Taylor (11)	134
Zac Glenn (9)	88	Hajra Razzaq (10)	135
Oskar Purlys (8)	89	Lola Wilmshurst (11)	136
Lucy Henry (8)	90	Caitlyn Todman (12)	137
Charles Bremner (8)	91	Jack Fraser (10)	138
Rhys Finlay (8)	92	Lewis Greig (11)	139
Guy Thompson (9)	93	Emma Arnold (10)	140
Jack McClelland (8)	94	Madeline Asher (11)	141
Reece Lavery (9)	95	Joseph Whyte (12)	142
		Struan Henderson (9)	143

Hartwell Primary School, Hartwell

Levi Cox (10)	96	Dylan Federico Ashe (10)	144
Katie Deller (10)	98	Kerr Kelso (8)	145
Pixie Czerniecki (10)	100	Connor Henderson (8)	146
Illy Wootton (10)	102	Jack Rees (9)	147
Jonathan Bark (10)	104	Benjamin Fraser (8)	148
Jessie Barby (10)	105	Jack Heath (8)	149
Jessica Ball (10)	106	Matthew Kay (10)	150
Amy Jewell (9)	108	Alfie Colgan (9)	151
Zac Gopole (9)	110	Blair Snedker (7)	152
Emma Banham-Hall (9)	111	Madison Park (10)	153
		Abigail Fraser (8)	154

Jack D'Sylva (9)	155
Leonie Kemp (10)	156
Liam Arnold (9)	157
Rylie Smart (8)	158
Jenna Heath (11)	159
Abigail Morton (8)	160
Ben Watson (10)	161
Coby Thomson (10)	162
Maia Harker (8)	163
Munroe Candlish (8)	164
Theerathan (8)	165
Kimberley Matysiak (10)	166
Rory Vaughan (7)	167
Cameron Ritchie (10)	168
Zoe Christie (8)	169
Iustin Pichiu (9)	170
Katy Arnold (7)	171

Millbrook Community Primary School, Kirkby

Sienna Pike (9)	172
Ethan Lundon (10)	174
Riley B V (9)	175
Ruby Lynskey (9)	176
Annie-Mai Brown (9)	177
Jacob Fisher (10)	178
Elizabeth Lewis (10)	179
Annie Browne (10)	180
Jasmine Jones (9)	181
Andrew James (10)	182
Lewis Doran (10)	183

Millbrook School, Cheshunt

Yue Yang (9)	184
Laura Yu (9)	185
Arjed Brooks-Taberos (9)	186
Kara Williams (9)	187
Zuzanna Michalowska (9)	188
Lydia Toms (8)	189
Poppy-Rose Irons (9)	190
Tara Brown-Anderson (9)	191
Rubie Crouch (9)	192

Fletcher Killingback (8)	193
Naomi Igboanusi (9)	194
Dempsey Wilson (9)	195
Joao Antonio Almeida (8)	196
Aidan Paterson (8)	197
Kyle Craig (9)	198

Ravensden CE Primary Academy, Ravensden

Alex Sawyer (10)	199
Summer Upshaw (11)	200
Ella Southam (11)	201
Leo Bell (9)	202
Zachary Dunn (9)	203
Ethan Richard Murgatroyd (10)	204
Jacob Shufflebotham (11)	205
Valentino Alessi (11)	206
Paige Davenport (10)	207

St Bridget's Primary RC School, Baillieston

Gabriella Peters (11)	208
Paige Logan (11)	210
Zoe Shek (12)	212
Ciara Tracy (11)	213
Andrew Provan (12)	214
Ava Curran (12)	215
Sophia Smith (12)	216

St Mary's Hampton CE Primary School, Hampton

Lucas Freeman (9)	217
Pavalan Nursimloo (10)	218
Israela Adeyoju (10)	222
Poppy Halpin (9)	225
Lois Luyombya (10)	226
Aliana Protopapa-Marnoch (10)	228
Bibi Roisin Adams (9)	229
Oliver Tattam (10)	230
Amelia Veasey (10)	231
Ivy George (9)	232

Zoe Brown (8)   233
India Howard (9)   234
Dilakshika Shanmaganathan (9)   235
Sophie McCann (9)   236
Mikayla Aimer (10)   237
Holly Griffin (10)   238
Romilly Heywood (10)   239
William Parish (8)   240
James Hannan (10)   241
Briar McKenna (10)   242
Dez Kordyl (9)   243
Maddie Bissett (8)   244
Vivienne Dzhikova (9)   245
Drake Sequeira (10)   246
Lauren Woods (10)   247
Kareena Mahl (9)   248

The Glasgow Academy, Kelvinbridge

Rachel Wyllie (11)   249
Milly Tabor Nunn (10)   250
Laura Humphreys (10)   251
Lexi Mitchell (10)   252
Erin Thomson (11)   253

Townhill Primary School, Townhill

Eden Murray (12)   254
C Bosshardt (9)   255

THE POEMS

COME ON SLOW COACH

Shape-Shifting Snow Leopard

Some people think snow leopards are bloodthirsty creatures,
Which have soft, white skin,
But not this snow leopard,
This one won Britain's Got Talent,
This one is a TV pop star.
It's not bloodthirsty, it's a vegetarian.
It has an underground lair
So it can have alone time.
It won a swimming contest.
It can speak any language in the world.
Spent one year and a month in the Mir in space.
Works with a secret agent koala.
This snow leopard can shape-shift.
It may not be a human
So don't be fooled by what you see.
It may be a snow leopard you wait and see!

Chrissie Chitura (8)
Abington Vale Primary School, Northampton

My Snow Leopard

S ilent, snowy snow leopard prowls his land.

N ot full but not hungry. Watch out! He's ready for a meal.

O n a tree, prey is spotted.

W ith prey in mind, no one can stop him.

L ittle do you know, this normally snowy fellow is quite black

E asy to spot, the prey starts to run but just

O n time, his mate arrives to catch a feast

P repare for action! The predators strike!

A ll are full after the kill

R eady to sleep, they have a nap

D are you to wake them up.

Caitlin Hughes (9)
Abington Vale Primary School, Northampton

Smelly Boots

Most people think Karl eats hamburgers all day
but those people are wrong.
Once Karl has finished his breakfast
he leaves the house and travels around the world
in a giant wellington boot.
He goes to England and eats some fish and chips
then he enjoys curries in India
and in Italy he devours fresh cheesy pizza.
But the strange thing is that no one,
not even Donald Trump
asks why a koala is travelling the world
in a giant wellington boot.
Somehow he gets home
in time to eat his favourite dinner - hamburgers.

Celesani Bhebe (9)
Abington Vale Primary School, Northampton

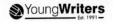

The Sneaky Snake

A snake is usually a violent hunter.
An animal that lives on land.
It would grab its prey and never let go.

But this snake is different.
Every night it sneaks out the house.
It triples in size.
Its scaly skin grows turquoise and knobbly.
Its eyes start to twinkle like an amber jewel.
It shoots out lasers from its mouth.
It slithers into space and eats satellites
And in the morning it slithers back home
And gets into my bedroom
As the sun starts to rise.

Tomorrow the next adventure begins.

Orla Collis (9)
Abington Vale Primary School, Northampton

The Hog

You all know hedgehogs...
Cute, not-so-cuddly little critters.
Well, my pet, no my companion is a hedgehog.
When running he sees in slo-mo
Because when sprinting his maximum speed is quadruple light speed.
He loves to eat and is great with things like tech.
Basically a hacker!
He can sense when something bad is about to happen.
My companion's name is Sadow.
He has similar powers to my favourite game, Sonic
And in Sonic there is a character called Shadow.
Sonic and Shadow together is Sadow.

Kenzo Bain (9)
Abington Vale Primary School, Northampton

Snowy The Snow Owl

People see Snowy as a pillow,
A soft, adorable and innocent little snow owl
As she walks around eating pancakes all day,
But in real life this owl is real trouble.
She is the most wanted, sneaky criminal,
As she lurks through the shadows,
Stealing from banks and attacking random people,
With her partner in crime, Vicious the puppy,
They are unstoppable.
Snowy has ocean-blue eyes and snowy-white fur.
So if you see this owl on the street,
Don't be blind, she's a criminal!

Maja Kusnierek (9)
Abington Vale Primary School, Northampton

The Cato

People think cats are cute, small, fast and have
soft skin
But this one is as big as a skyscraper
And it jumps as high as a skyscraper.
Not scared of water at all.
When it's hungry it goes to a beach
And goes into the ocean to have supper,
Supper is blue whale and shark.
This cat is a superhero.
It stomps on the most ferocious villains in town
Then gets arrested and gets put in the most secure
prison on Earth.

Abraham Zahran (8)
Abington Vale Primary School, Northampton

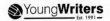

The Basketball Parrot

He glides down the street on a navy blue board.
He has lime green feathers and feet that are clawed.
He pulls up at the court and begins to fly.
He does a slam dunk and cries, "Easy as pie!"
He has crimson framed shades and a midnight-blue cap.
He pats the competitor, "What a chap!"
He leaves us bewildered, shocked, without a clue!
Then one of my friends says, "That parrot belongs to you!"

Ben Hateley (9)
Abington Vale Primary School, Northampton

The Linake

A snake that can hack?
Bet you've never seen that!
This sneaky snake would slither into your room
And could put you to impeccable doom!
A lion's body,
Laser eyes.
Invisible wings that will make you cry.
If you hear a rattle, don't cry!
Just get out of your house at the speed of light.
Venom in his fangs,
Can burrow.
Look under your bed
To make sure you're not being followed.

Lola Newman (8)
Abington Vale Primary School, Northampton

The Cag

By day it is your normal cute cat
But at night it is something else,
Half-cat, half-dog put together.
It breathes fire
So you better watch out!
It runs at the speed of light
And eats 1,000 McDonald's cheeseburgers
And washes it down with delicious chocolate
milkshakes.
I must not forget to say...
It is as big as a house with fiery red wings
And lasers that shoot out of his eyes.

Myles Houghton (9)
Abington Vale Primary School, Northampton

Brownie The Monkey

Jumping from building to building is the dance
fighting monkey.
Brownie's her name.
When you are dancing with her you'll always feel
the shame.
People crowd around
When she's showing off her fame.
She snuggles in for a cuddle
To show you she's tame.
She plays Hungry Hippos and Splat!
But Twister is her favourite game.
She once met the Queen
Who made her a dame.

Sophie Winston (8)
Abington Vale Primary School, Northampton

Princess Tapper

I can tap, I can dance,
I am a tap superstar.
I have a pretty pink tutu
And shiny tap hooves,
I love the pink ribbon in my hair.
I am a pretty pink unicorn.
I am not really, I am a princess pink horse
But I have a tall, colourful horn like a unicorn
So I pretend to be a unicorn.
My mum said she would sign me up
For Britain's Got Talent
To show off my tap talent.

Phoebe Wingrove (9)
Abington Vale Primary School, Northampton

Camo The Chameleon

Some people think chameleons are rough and
scaly,
That they are green and quite big.
Some people think they can't talk,
But not this one...
It's blue and has a tail like a rainbow.
It can fly and knows how to work a gun.
It's super strong and it's never missed a shot.
He's a secret agent working for the government.
His name is Camo the chameleon.

Iggy Thurlow (9)
Abington Vale Primary School, Northampton

The Criminal White Tiger

You might think the white tiger is cuddly
But it is very dangerous.
He hacks computers,
He can turn into a person.
He has razor-sharp teeth.
He is a very good spy criminal.
He is too good at killing people.

He is very sneaky.
He is faster than the speed of light.
He has a black suit.
But just know that this tiger is different to other
white tigers.

Joseph Kanguni (8)
Abington Vale Primary School, Northampton

Dangerous Dolphin

Midnight-blue eyes stare into the distance.
Just then out comes a large body that shoots up
like a rocket and zooms back down.
A big sandstorm appears as the dolphin lands.
Now this dolphin is very unusual,
Suddenly it disappears.
It appears again.
Did you know this animal can camouflage?
So watch out,
it could be in your house spying on you!

Siyona Patel (8)
Abington Vale Primary School, Northampton

Slither The Snake

You probably think a snake is small, calm
And always stays in a box
And when it gets scared it will bite you.

But this snake isn't scared,
It never goes in a box.
He isn't small.
He works with his partner, Sage the bat.
They fight crime together.
They never ever surrender and always win.
This snake is a secret agent.

Emily Bignell (9)
Abington Vale Primary School, Northampton

Technology Tiger

You may think tigers are feisty and lazy.
Also, they're so cuddly.
However, this tiger is different.
This tiger is good at fixing electronics.
It's black and has white ears.
His favourite food is a phone.
He can tell if you need help with fixing your electronics.
Also, it can talk to you.
This is a technology tiger!

Heer Patel (8)
Abington Vale Primary School, Northampton

Adorable Duck

A ctive

D uck

O r

R avenous.

A ngry if it sees a

B ucket full of

L uck

E ven though he

D oesn't have luck

U nlike a

C at which lands on its feet and

K icks about.

Maximilian Kufuor (9)
Abington Vale Primary School, Northampton

My Pet Tarantula

Some people think tarantulas are scary
They can bite
They can fight
They can really give you a fright

But my tarantula is no ordinary tarantula
She's a cutie
Such a beauty
And instead of shooting hairs, she shoots gummy bears!

Lacey Tilley (8)
Abington Vale Primary School, Northampton

The Holiday Horse

H at and umbrella, she shelters from the heat.
O n a sunbed by a beautiful swimming pool.
R elaxing with a glass of piña colada.
S unbathing in a resort in Barbados.
E very horse would be jealous of this.

Isla Hallett (9)
Abington Vale Primary School, Northampton

Pesky Penguin

It is very naughty
And sneaky.
As small as a ball.
Its webbed feet make it wobble
And it's not very tall.
Its feathers are grey
And its beak is orange.
It takes all my stuff
When I'm not looking.

Lex Tilley (8)
Abington Vale Primary School, Northampton

Long Neck

It has red skin like blood.
It is as long as a train, like HS2.
It has 100 claws on each hand, blood-covered.
Its scales are long.
It's really fast, like ten times faster than lightning.

What is it?

Oli Forbes (9)
Abington Vale Primary School, Northampton

Clever Crayfish

Crayfish here, crayfish there, crayfish almost everywhere
Claws snapping in the air
Blues to camouflage in the crystal water
Reds to say, "Stay away!"
If you see him, you'll be stunned!

Jack Brennan (8)
Abington Vale Primary School, Northampton

No Ordinary Horse

White as snow.
He is only young so he is small.
Lightning-fast.
Skillfully crosses the ball.
Plays for Liverpool.
Dark blue eyes
And no ordinary horse.

Noah Parker (8)
Abington Vale Primary School, Northampton

Triple Trouble

As long as a football pitch.
As tall as ten buses.
Crimson-red eyes.
Sharp, poisonous fangs.
As fast as light.
Smelly breath.

What am I?

Andrew McGourty (9)
Abington Vale Primary School, Northampton

Batraf

B atraf is very cool he likes going in the pool

A pples he likes along with bikes and long hikes

T ag he plays for many days with many friends

R abbits he chases for hours and hours he chipped his tooth on a tile

A t night he tries to fight but he doesn't fight

F un he's had but he thinks he has had the best day ever.

Robbie Thomson (11)

Banchory Primary School, Tullibody

Gerrard The Griffin

My pet Gerrard the griffin he's a very special pet.
When it is hot he goes outside and sweats.
He has lot of scales.
Which almost broke my mum's nails.
Sometimes he is lazy.
But he can be crazy.

Kyle Bryce (11)
Banchory Primary School, Tullibody

Bob The Dog

I've got a dog called Bob
Bob is very dotty
But my friend calls him Motty
My friend came over
"Hello Motty"
"It's Dotty not Motty"
His real name is Bob anyway!

Charlie Edwards (11)
Banchory Primary School, Tullibody

Rar The Fat Dog

Rar the dog is so fat
He can't even fit through a door
He is almost the size of a cow
Rar is as silly as a sausage
Rar loves his maw she is so braw
He loves his dad unless he is mad.

Keira-Angel Hammond (11)
Banchory Primary School, Tullibody

Billy The Hippo

B eware the putrid smell of Billy the hippopotamus

I ncapable of swimming

L azy as a donkey

L oud like a sheep

Y ou've *never* seen anything quite like him!

Katherine Bowie (12)
Banchory Primary School, Tullibody

The Actor's Lion Monkey

The actor's lion monkey is an adventurous, attractive lion monkey.
The actor's lion monkey is a bossy, brave lion monkey.
The actor's lion monkey is a courageous, curious lion monkey.

The ballerina's lion monkey is a daring, daydreaming lion monkey.
The ballerina's lion monkey is an eager, elegant lion monkey.
The ballerina's lion monkey is a feisty, fluffy lion monkey.

Cleo's lion monkey is a gnawing, golden lion monkey.
Cleo's lion monkey is a hilarious, happy lion monkey.
Cleo's lion monkey is an inventing, incredible lion monkey.

Daisy's lion monkey is a joking, jolly lion monkey.
Daisy's lion monkey is a kind, kissing lion monkey.
Daisy's lion monkey is a linguistic, language-speaking lion monkey.

Saffron Howell (10)
Erpingham CE Primary School, Erpingham

Beth's Rabbit

Beth's rabbit is an adorable, adventurous and astounding rabbit.
Beth's rabbit is a brilliant, busy rabbit.
Beth's rabbit is a confident, cheerful and courageous rabbit.

The teacher's rabbit is a determined, dizzy and disturbed rabbit.
The teacher's rabbit is an elegant, excitable and eager rabbit.
The teacher's rabbit is a fantastic, filthy and fast rabbit.

Rose's rabbit is a glamorous, gleaming and great rabbit.
Rose's rabbit is a happy, helpful and healthy rabbit.
Rose's rabbit is an inventive, intelligent and inquisitive rabbit.

The dancer's rabbit is a jumpy, jolly and joyful rabbit.
The dancer's rabbit is a kind, keen and knowing rabbit.

The dancer's rabbit is a lovely, long and leaping rabbit.

Poppy's rabbit is a magical, modern and marvellous rabbit.
Poppy's rabbit is a nice, natural and naughty rabbit.
Poppy's rabbit is an optimistic, operatic and open rabbit.

The farmer's rabbit is a pretty, permanent and precious rabbit.
The farmer's rabbit is a quick, queasy and quiet rabbit.
The farmer's rabbit is a revolting, responsible and restless rabbit.

Violet's rabbit is a super, speedy and stealthy rabbit.
Violet's rabbit is a thirsty, thin and thoughtful rabbit.
Violet's rabbit is an unwell, unique and unhappy rabbit.

The doctor's rabbit is a valuable, vegan and vain rabbit.
The doctor's rabbit is a well-known, wet and wide rabbit.
The doctor's rabbit is an X-raying and xylophoning rabbit.

Daisy's rabbit is a yo-yoing, yellow rabbit.
Daisy's rabbit is a zippy, zoomy rabbit.

Beth Catleugh (10)
Erpingham CE Primary School, Erpingham

Kris' Dog

Kris' dog is an amazing dog.
Kris' dog is a beautiful dog.
Kris' dog is a cute dog.

Mum's dog is a dangerous dog.
Mum's dog is an energetic dog.
Mum's dog is a fun dog.

Dad's dog is a great dog.
Dad's dog is a hunting dog.
Dad's dog is an inquisitive dog.

Nan's dog is a jumping dog.
Nan's dog is a kissing dog.
Nan's dog is a lucky dog.

Grandad's dog is a monstrous dog.
Grandad's dog is a snoring dog.
Grandad's dog is an obstinate dog.

Kris Chapman (11)
Erpingham CE Primary School, Erpingham

Lily-Beth's Pony

Lily-Beth's pony is an amazing, adorable and active pony.
Lily-Beth's pony is a brilliant, bouncy and busy pony.
Lily-Beth's pony is a curious, cunning and creative pony.

The doctor's pony is a dirty, dizzy and delightful pony.
The doctor's pony is an eager, excellent and epic pony.
The doctor's pony is a funny, fearful and fluffy pony.

The teacher's pony is a gigantic, gorgeous and great pony.
The teacher's pony is a hungry, happy and healthy pony.
The teacher's pony is an intelligent, inventive and incredible pony.

The postman's pony is a joyful, jolly and jiggly pony.
The postman's pony is a kind, knowing and kissing pony.
The postman's pony is a loving, lonely and lost pony.

Ava's pony is a magnificent, magical and mad pony.
Ava's pony is a noisy, napping and new pony.
Ava's pony is an open, operatic and odd pony.

Mary's pony is a patient, perfect and precious pony.
Mary's pony is a quiet, quick and quarrelling pony.
Mary's pony is a remarkable, reliant and respectable pony.

The policeman's pony is a skipping, soft and selfish pony.
The policeman's pony is a tall, tame and terrified pony.
The policeman's pony is an unhappy, ungrateful and unique pony.

The student's pony is a vicious, violent and vegetarian pony.
The student's pony is a worried, wealthy and well-known pony.
The student's pony is a xylophoning X-ray pony.

The scientist's pony is a young, yellow and yearning pony.
The scientist's pony is a zebra-like, zooming pony.

Lily-Beth Hollinger (10)
Erpingham CE Primary School, Erpingham

Tyler's Sloth

Tyler's sloth is an adorable sloth.
Tyler's sloth is a beautiful sloth.
Tyler's sloth is a cute sloth.

Max's sloth is a dangerous sloth.
Max's sloth is an engineering sloth.
Max's sloth is a fun sloth.

Mitchell's sloth is a gorgeous sloth.
Mitchell's sloth is a happy sloth.
Mitchell's sloth is an ingenious sloth.

Tyler Fenton (9)
Erpingham CE Primary School, Erpingham

Esme's Dog

Esme's dog is an adorable, amorous and anxious dog.
Esme's dog is a beautiful, brilliant and boastful dog.
Esme's dog is a curious, confident and clumsy dog.

The teacher's dog is a desperate, disturbed and disgusted dog.
The teacher's dog is an eager, energetic and excited dog.
The teacher's dog is a furious, forgetful and fantastic dog.

Mum's dog is a gorgeous, gleaming and grumpy dog.
Mum's dog is a helpful, healthy and hungry dog.
Mum's dog is an intelligent, ice-skating dog.

Lucy's dog is a joyful, jolly and jittery dog.
Lucy's dog is a kind, kicking and keen dog.
Lucy's dog is a lucky, lovely and loveable dog.

Dad's dog is a modern, magnificent and mad dog.
Dad's dog is a nice, native and natural dog.
Dad's dog is an observant, obsessed and optimistic dog.

Bailey's dog is a pretty, particular and precious dog.
Bailey's dog is a quiet, quick and queasy dog.
Bailey's dog is a reliable, regular and rapid dog.

The doctor's dog is a super, slow and silent dog.
The doctor's dog is a trippy, truthful and tricky dog.
The doctor's dog is an underrated, useful and unique dog.

The fireman's dog is a valuable, vain and victorious dog.
The fireman's dog is a wonderful, warsome and wicked dog.
The fireman's dog is an X-ray dog.

April's dog is a yapping, yelling and young dog.
April's dog is a zappy, zooming and zig-zagging dog.

Esme Marling (10)
Erpingham CE Primary School, Erpingham

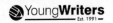

The Wrights' Dinosaurs

The Wrights' dinosaur is an adorable dinosaur.
The Wrights' dinosaur is a bossy dinosaur.
The Wrights' dinosaur is a cute dinosaur.

Summer's dinosaur is a dipstick dinosaur.
Summer's dinosaur is an empty dinosaur.
Summer's dinosaur is a furry dinosaur.

Steve P's dinosaur is a ginormous dinosaur.
Steve P's dinosaur is a horrendous dinosaur.
Steve P's dinosaur is an intelligent dinosaur.

Mitchell's dinosaur is a jagged dinosaur.
Mitchell's dinosaur is a keen dinosaur.
Mitchell's dinosaur is a lazy dinosaur.

LBH's dinosaur is a magnificent dinosaur.
LBH's dinosaur is a noble dinosaur.
LBH's dinosaur is an obedient dinosaur.

Lilly's dinosaur is a patient dinosaur.
Lilly's dinosaur is a quiet dinosaur.
Lilly's dinosaur is a raging dinosaur.

Daniella's dinosaur is a sarcastic dinosaur.
Daniella's dinosaur is a terrific dinosaur.
Daniella's dinosaur is a unique dinosaur.

Nicole's dinosaur is a vain dinosaur.
Nicole's dinosaur is a wandering dinosaur.
Nicole's dinosaur is an 'xcited dinosaur.

Beth's dinosaur is a yelping dinosaur.
Beth's dinosaur is a zooming dinosaur.

Kayden Wright (9)
Erpingham CE Primary School, Erpingham

Alaina's Snow Leopard

Alaina's snow leopard is an adorable, astonishing and amazing snow leopard.
Alaina's snow leopard is a bossy, beautiful snow leopard.
Alaina's snow leopard is a clumsy, clear-minded, confident snow leopard.

The zoo's snow leopard is determined and dizzy.
The zoo's snow leopard is enormous, excited and elephant-like.
The zoo's snow leopard is fiery-eyed and fire-breathing.

Tallulah's snow leopard is gaining, gaming and gassy.
Tallulah's snow leopard is hulky, hairy and ham-eating.
Tallulah's snow leopard is icy, ignorant and imitating.

Lilly's snow leopard is jagged-toothed and jealous.
Lilly's snow leopard is kind, karaoke-loving and kicking.
Lilly's snow leopard is lamb-eating, Labrador-like and lanky.

Summer's snow leopard is mad, macaroni-loving and musical.
Summer's snow leopard is naughty, nosy and necklace-like.
Summer's snow leopard is obedient, obnoxious and occupied.

Beth's snow leopard is pale, pacy and pampered.
Beth's snow leopard is quarrelling, questioning and quiet.
Beth's snow leopard is a racer, red and rocky.

The baby snow leopard is skeleton-turning, sensible and sacred.

Alaina Bray (10)
Erpingham CE Primary School, Erpingham

Cameron's Dog

Cameron's dog is an adorable and athletic dog.
Cameron's dog is a barking and bonkers dog.
Cameron's dog is a cute and confident dog.

Cameron Carter-Lee (10)

Erpingham CE Primary School, Erpingham

Tomas The Rainbow Turtle

T omas the rainbow turtle is as marvellous as can be
O h I want to see my friends and family
M arvellous as my family
A s colourful as a rainbow
S ometimes it can be lazy like me

T imes it can be sassy which is funny, I can see
H uggles are my favourite just like ice cream
E ating ice cream is my favourite thing

T imes I can go fast, times I can go slow
U nder the sea is where I love to be
R unning is hard and swimming is easy
T oday I was with my family
L oving and always caring for y friends and family
E veryone is loving and caring for everybody.

Chloe Adams (7)
Fort Hill Integrated Primary School, Lisburn

Candy The Magic Unicorn

One day a girl walking
Wished she had a unicorn
But then the whole place turned rainbow
She was so amazed then a unicorn appeared
Wow!
The little girl said, "A unicorn!"
She ran so fast she was at Daisy's house in a flash
She ran in. "Daisy!"
"What?" Daisy said
"Come down."
Daisy came. "Wow!"
Daisy said, "A unicorn!
Can we ride it?"
"Yep," the little girl said
"Amazing," said Daisy
So they set off to candy land
They made it
Daisy and the little girl got sticky
But Candy's magic washed it all off
Yay!

Lucy Jelly (8)
Fort Hill Integrated Primary School, Lisburn

Leafy Just Leafy...

This is Cloud Cuckoo Land
Where you can find your favourite leafy
Leafys look like angel cats
Not sure why they have horns
But hey it makes them look cute
Weird how they know when predators are coming
Just from a halo like a lightbulb
Well I'm lost about things to say about leafys
Wait don't stop reading
If you were in Australia
You could see the magic if you were in America
That's all I can say about leafys, not all alien
Leafys are as fluffy as clouds
Shiny as a star
Priceless like £1,000,000
I'm having a really fun time
That's really all I can say about leafys.

Jackson Smith (8)
Fort Hill Integrated Primary School, Lisburn

Rainbow Kitsune

R eally fluffy, furry pet.
A dorable rainbow creature that loves to eat rainbows.
I n the Internet you can't find it!
N ASA thinks it's an alien,
B ut I believe it's not!
O h my, everything is covered in rainbow drink!
W hat a good, playful pet.

K itty or wolf? I don't care
I just care about my fluffy friend
T he most colourful friend you've seen.
S ome say it's not real, but I have one.
U nder my bed is where it sleeps.
N ice and soft under there.
E very day we play and jump. We love it.

Ala Pieniak (9)
Fort Hill Integrated Primary School, Lisburn

The Spy Sloth

Spy Sloth loves to write
The pig stole potatoes from Mrs Bird
The cat hissed
The dog was playing with a ball
Clabong! Clabong!
So the cat attacked the pig
Spy Sloth stopped it
The next morning Spy Sloth was spying
On piggy, he was getting a mask.
But it was not like a cool mask
It was like Spy Sloth
But he knew that it was a copy
The next morning *bang, bang!*
Spy Sloth woke up
It was Mrs Bird and Chicken Little
Piggy stole from Spy Sloth
Mrs Bird was crying
But Spy Sloth was spying
And Piggy went to jail, yay!

Sofia Smith (8)
Fort Hill Integrated Primary School, Lisburn

The Chickcorn

Chickcorn hates dogs because his owner wants one.
He loves going to England
So he gets to see Terry, his owner's mum's dog.
Its horn is bigger than an elephant's trunk.
Chickcorn's favourite food is ice cream.
King Kong is his favourite movie.
Chocolate eggs come out every day.
Orange is his favourite colour
But he turns green when he gets sad.
Ralph the frog also turns green
So he won't get bullied at animal training.
Nutella is his best friend, she's a squirrel.

Caleb McCready (9)
Fort Hill Integrated Primary School, Lisburn

Dino Dog

D oggy Dino is the only doggy with dino spikes.

I t turns into a dino at night and its prey is bats.

N ot only does Doggy Dino turn into a dino he also has a mouth like a fish.

O n Dino Doggy's birthday he has a servant that hunts bats and he turns them into a bat cake.

D ino Doggy loves drinking bats' blood.

O n the weekend he goes out to hang out with his dino friends to go hunting for bats.

G oing to head out now. Dino Doggy has signed out.

Chloe McCormick (9)
Fort Hill Integrated Primary School, Lisburn

Mad Superhero Mango's Life

My pet is called Mad Superhero Mango.
Her favourite song is Tuesday Tango.
She is a very cute cat
That sleeps on a mat.
Mad Superhero Mango is a stray
But every day she goes to the park to play.
Her birthday is in May.
She sleeps in a box, that's where she stays.
But one day she went for a swim
But she got pulled in the waterfall and fell down.
It was 10,000 feet tall so, all of a sudden,
She flew up into the air with her flying power
And landed in a huge flower!

Lillie McLoughlin (8)
Fort Hill Integrated Primary School, Lisburn

The Tiny Pink And Blue Pup

T iny as it can be
I t's also very cute
N ever aggressive
Y es it's very fluffy

P olite as possible
I ncredible as can be
N ot rude but sometimes grumpy
K ind as it can be

B onds with anyone
L oving as a kitten
U nstoppable as can be
E ats a lot

P ink as candyfloss
U nbeatable
P ies are her favourite to eat.

Katie Murray (8)
Fort Hill Integrated Primary School, Lisburn

Jumping Jet

J umping Jet is my pet.

U nder the quilt Jet sleeps.

M idnight he leaps out of bed.

P roud of his jet-black coat.

I nto the outside he runs then he comes home.

N ever feed him chips or he'll spit them out.

G et him a rope and play tug-of-war.

J et loves eating cheese.

E very day he makes his eyes glow.

T ry to see him when it's dark, it will be hard.

Matthew Simpson (9)

Fort Hill Integrated Primary School, Lisburn

Jinxasorys And Me!

J inxasorys is as cute as a puppy
I s as soft as a kitten
N ice as a koala baby
X marks the spot, she would love to be a pirate
A s colourful as a rainbow
S o so excitable as a puppy
O h she's in a huff, *stomp stomp,* the ground shakes
R *oar, roar* she is so excited for cuddles
Y ou are so special to me
S he is asleep in her bed, sweet dreams.

Imogen Champness-Curran (8)
Fort Hill Integrated Primary School, Lisburn

All About Dogion

D ogion looks like a standard dog, his favourite food is a frog.

O f course, he is special, he has a wrecking ball on his tail and he has jump boots that make him sail!

G reen food he loves, he is very cold all the time so he wears gloves.

I t turns into a lion at night and hunts frogs.

O n his birthday he gets his family to hunt frogs for him and he makes a cake out of it.

N et worth is 7.2 million pounds.

Thomas Calinski (9)

Fort Hill Integrated Primary School, Lisburn

Slimy Ellie

S he is a pet that's cute and slimy.
L ittle Ellie is as cute as a puppy.
I t is a slimy queen that puts people on fire.
M agical slime oozes everywhere.
Y ou could slip on the slime easily.

E llie has hypnotic powers.
L oves to put people in trances.
L ittle Ellie loves to mess.
I s leaving a huge slimy path.
E arly in the morning she loves flying.

Leina Johnston (8)
Fort Hill Integrated Primary School, Lisburn

General Ginger

G eneral Ginger is gigantic
E xtraordinarily clever
N ever does anything bad
E ats cat food
R uns around all the time
A lways loves walking in the rain
L aughs all the time

G rowls like a lion
I s as crazy as a cat
N ever goes to bed on time
G rumpy in the mornings
E xercises all day long
R estless in the dark.

Callum Elder (8)
Fort Hill Integrated Primary School, Lisburn

Rocky And Me

Rocky and me went to a lake, it was beautiful and
shiny
Rocky jumped in *splish, splosh*
Then he had to go back to work
He sells ice cream
His favourite flavour is chocolate
He always comes to me for cuddles
His favourite game is catch the ball
He can also speak human language
He is so fast at running
He can also get bored and do crazy stuff
He also flies at night *swoosh swoosh.*

Alice Gray (7)
Fort Hill Integrated Primary School, Lisburn

Weird And Bob

W eird is Bob's mum's name. Bob is a baby, they are both monkeys.

E very day Weird gets Bob from nursery.

I n Bob's world everything is huge.

R eally amazing.

D id you know Weird and Bob like to eat birds.

B ob likes to hang on trees.

O n Friday Bob and Weird are lazy.

B ad days are when Bob and Weird split up and can't find each other.

Charley Kirkpatrick (9)
Fort Hill Integrated Primary School, Lisburn

Mr Tiny Tim

M y pet can turn into a huge turtle.
R eally amazing in every way.

T he turtle can time travel.
I t eats carrots and lettuce.
N ight-time he hunts for food.
Y ou'd better watch out, he likes to eat humans.

T iny Tim is very, very angry.
I s a little turtle until it turns into a giant turtle.
M y pet is amazing.

Lily Dougherty (9)
Fort Hill Integrated Primary School, Lisburn

Rampage Of Dogzilla!

The sun has gone down
The nocturnal beast was awakened
Dogzilla was on a rampage
Kaboom! Kaboom!
Dogzilla was mercilessly breaking car windows
Smash! goes a window. *Boom!*
A car exploded!
Smash! A building fell over.
Ahhh! People were screaming
Super Biscuit is dead because of dogzilla
Dawn is approaching
She is going to sleep!

Alex Korbik (8)
Fort Hill Integrated Primary School, Lisburn

Super Budgie

S uper Budgie can fly very fast
U p high in the sky
P layful as a kitten
E ats sunflower seeds
R uffled feathers when he's cold

B rave as a lion
U nbelievably strong lifting the tree out of the ground
D eadly to other animals
G entle with his friends
I ncredibly fast
E very day he flies.

Oliver Fulton (8)

Fort Hill Integrated Primary School, Lisburn

Dinodog

Dinodog is usually found at the ruin of an asteroid.
Or in a hole where 20 or 30 dinosaur bones are
found.
Don't go close or he'll attack.
His spine charges fireballs.
They shoot from his mouth.
One fireball nearly hit my drone.
For defence the spikes on his tail and back glow
orange.
His skin is usually dark green
But at night at 1am he glows bright green.

Joel Tait (8)
Fort Hill Integrated Primary School, Lisburn

Hi! Let Me Tell You About Libby

She is very lazy
And would eat anything - even a daisy!
Every day she walks on her ears
And takes away a little child's tears.
Every day she takes a five-hour nap.
She also loves eating snacks.
She used to think she had no purpose
Until she got offered work in a circus.
Now she gets treats and money every day.
That's all about Libby for today.

Taylor Gray (9)
Fort Hill Integrated Primary School, Lisburn

My Peculiar Pet Dragoncorn

D ragoncorn can fly.

R eally nice.

A t night my dragoncorn mane turns into fire.

G o on an adventure with me.

O n the way we will stop for pizza for tea!

N ow isn't that nice?

C ome on.

O h we are, ready to go.

R eally, wasn't that wonderful?

N ow let's go home and say bye-bye.

Rosie-Anne McGrath (8)
Fort Hill Integrated Primary School, Lisburn

Rocco The Runt

R occo is a French bulldog that flies with his ears.

O n the 4th of September he drank some beers and said cheers.

C oconuts are Rocco's favourite food and he is very rude.

C oconuts are good for Rocco's lion-sized stomach and they stop him from being sick when he is flying.

O llie the ostrich is Rocco's best friend.

Brody McFarland (9)
Fort Hill Integrated Primary School, Lisburn

Jazzy Jef The Falcon

J ef is as crazy as a monkey
A jazzy falcon he is
Z ooms through the sky so fast and high
Z ooming past the people he's nothing
Y awning as I say goodnight

J et likes a fly around in the morning
E ating our lunch as I see him munching away
F un and Jazzy Jef is very special to me.

Sam Naga (8)
Fort Hill Integrated Primary School, Lisburn

Kittycorn's Powers And Favourite Foods

K ittycorn is as fast as a panther
I s never lazy any day
T iny and gigantic without trouble
T winkling sparkles shine like a star
Y ummy food in every meal
C arrots and apples with
O range so juicy as sweets
R unning and leaping very very fast
N othing will beat Kittycorn.

Abigail Kennedy (8)
Fort Hill Integrated Primary School, Lisburn

Why Are Drittens So Rare?

D rittens are very rare,

R arer than diamonds.

I n their minds the world seems to be a disgrace.

T hey have scales nearly everywhere and each is worth one million pounds.

T hey are half-dragon and half-kitten.

E very day they are hunted and killed.

N early all of them are extinct.

Abigail Heaney (9)
Fort Hill Integrated Primary School, Lisburn

Nibblescorn

N ever gives up
I ncredible and so cute
B etter than everything
B elieves everything
L ucky as anything
E ats rainbows and loves unicorns
S uper cute
C lever as can be
O utside he loves
R ainbows are his favourite
N ibbles on carrots.

Helena Parker (8)
Fort Hill Integrated Primary School, Lisburn

Firey Breathes Fire

F irey likes fire, he even lives in it. He eats ashes and breathes fire.

I t is a lion. Every night he gets warmer because of the fire.

R oddy is one of his friends. He doesn't go near him because Firey got kicked out of the zoo.

E legant. He's very elegant.

Y ou should never make him angry.

Ethan Edgar-McAleenon (8)

Fort Hill Integrated Primary School, Lisburn

Trantranv

T arantula he is.

R ents a tank.

A t home he is insane.

N et worth is 1.7 billion worth of vodka.

T rantranv is so big.

R eally hates Donald Trump.

A t home it is so hot.

N o one is allowed his vodka.

V odka makes him strong.

Oscar McCutcheon (9)
Fort Hill Integrated Primary School, Lisburn

Super Biscuit Returns!

Super strong and secret and is the best
He will be the fastest agent ever
Will he be able to save the UK?
Yes he will save all people in the UK
He's strong, brave and smart
He destroys buildings, cars and cities, *boom!*
Kaboom! A house is on fire, help!

Jack Meneary (8)
Fort Hill Integrated Primary School, Lisburn

Glowfur

I take Glowfur for walks every night.
It has glowing blue spots at night.
In the morning it is black with blue glowing eyes.
It sleeps outside on the grass.
He is like a cheetah.
I leave the window open so Glowfur jumps in.
He usually barks for food.
He eats bacon.

Fabko Budo (9)
Fort Hill Integrated Primary School, Lisburn

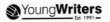

Jessie

J essie is a flying cat.

E very day he goes to China.

S ometimes Jessie likes to go to China to see his mum.

S ometimes Jessie flies to the shop to buy sweets.

I love Jessie, he is my favourite cat.

E ating is his favourite thing.

Blake Reid (9)

Fort Hill Integrated Primary School, Lisburn

Tim

Hi, my name is Tim.
I live in the rainforest.
My ceiling is a path.
I have a ladder so I can find food.
I can get bigger and faster.
I can run at 200mph.
At night I become invisible.
My teeth are as sharp as knives.
My teeth are four inches long.

Jake Duncan (8)
Fort Hill Integrated Primary School, Lisburn

Miracle Cat

J essie is the best cat ever

E veryone adores her

S omewhere in your heart you love her too

S he knows we love her very much

I n our house she adores us too

E veryone should know in our house there is never-ending love.

Georgia Friars (8)
Fort Hill Integrated Primary School, Lisburn

Meowery The Human Cat

M eowery is a rare species.

E veryone likes him.

O nly he can understand humans.

W e like to play with him.

E ven cats like him.

R ats are his favourite food.

Y ou should also know he won't hurt you.

Corey Currie (9)

Fort Hill Integrated Primary School, Lisburn

Magical Mandi's Marvellous Show

Mandi is a magical bat that does tricks and shows. Did you know at the end of his shows he bows and goes?
But anyway, I say I'm proud of him though.

M agical
A dorable
N oble
D aring
I ncredible.

Connie Green (9)
Fort Hill Integrated Primary School, Lisburn

Cupcake Is The Best

C upcake is very dangerous
U p and up she goes
P oor Cupcake gets sad sometimes
C upcake is very scary
A nd has wings and flies away
K ick the ball, there you go
E nd of the world she will destroy.

Jack Porter (8)
Fort Hill Integrated Primary School, Lisburn

Super Bug

S uper ladybug can climb walls
U ses mind powers
P aper planes I have under my shell
E nemies
R eaching to the skies

B ig ladybug coming your way
U ndefeatable
G reatest bug!

Carter Greer (7)
Fort Hill Integrated Primary School, Lisburn

Super Cat

S uperpowers has my cat
U p he flies
P unching the bad guys
E nemies beware!
R un away fast

C ats love him
A ll over town he goes
T ime for Super Cat to rest on his pillow.

Mason Duff-Dalzell (8)

Fort Hill Integrated Primary School, Lisburn

Lazy

L azy is a cat, he loves to play and sleep
A nd have a good time, he is a perfect pet to have, he likes
Z ebras, he loves books joy and his bed, he is a good pet.
Y ou would want him as a pet as you could have fun.

Amy Graham (8)
Fort Hill Integrated Primary School, Lisburn

Super Rabbit

Super Rabbit has a superhero habit.
He has gadgets on his back
And he takes the baddies back to base.
His dad went to space
To get a rock from Mars.
He brought it back
And put it on his back.

Alex Stevenson (9)
Fort Hill Integrated Primary School, Lisburn

Josh

J osh is part of an emergency team.

O ne day he saved a child from a burning building.

S ometimes he likes to fly to Japan to have sushi.

H e is a dog that flies like a helicopter.

Zac Glenn (9)

Fort Hill Integrated Primary School, Lisburn

The Amazing Cat

A lfie is furry like a fluffball
L azy like a sloth
F urry but adorable
I f he wants to sleep he will sleep in a tree
E ven if he falls off he will be okay.

Oskar Purlys (8)
Fort Hill Integrated Primary School, Lisburn

Unicorn

C ute as a puppy
U nbelievably smart
P uppies are cute
C olourful as a rainbow
A s cute as a giraffe
K ind as can be
E at all day.

Lucy Henry (8)
Fort Hill Integrated Primary School, Lisburn

Jakey My Deadly Pet!

J akey is as deadly as a python
A nd as fast as a leopard
K night in shining armour
E ats everything in its path
Y ells like a giant so be careful!

Charles Bremner (8)
Fort Hill Integrated Primary School, Lisburn

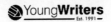

Fat Fox!

F at as a blue whale
A s nice as a puppy
T idy as a teacher

F unny as a baby
O utside in the sun
X mas dinner for you.

Rhys Finlay (8)
Fort Hill Integrated Primary School, Lisburn

Messy

M essy is a really fast dog.

E very day she runs a kilometre.

S he is nice.

S he is quick.

Y ou cannot catch her even if you try.

Guy Thompson (9)

Fort Hill Integrated Primary School, Lisburn

Rain The Cat

R ain likes to play like me
A t my house she likes lying in the sun
I n my house at night she can fly
N oisy like a monkey.

Jack McClelland (8)
Fort Hill Integrated Primary School, Lisburn

Jack

J ack is a flying hamster.
A ll day he flies in the sky.
C ome and see him in the air.
K ing of hamsters.

Reece Lavery (9)

Fort Hill Integrated Primary School, Lisburn

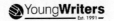

The Peculiar Half-Car, Half-Cat

Thunderously,
Beeping,
Glistening horn,
Cherry-red.

Deafeningly
Shrieking,
Boisterous honking,
Drowning out sounds.

Protectively
Shielding,
Aggressive outbursts,
Without warning.

Picky,
About munching,
Because
Of a heart-stopping nightmare.

Exclusive diet,
Specific sticks,
Jagged toothline.

Recklessly
Sprinting,
In a circle,
Audibly devours.

Multicoloured,
Rainbow,
Glimmers like the sun,
On a scorching afternoon.

Radiant
Stripes,
Gold, turquoise, red,
Museum worthy.

Rapidly
Changing,
Lugubrious moods,
Brightening your day.

Levi Cox (10)
Hartwell Primary School, Hartwell

Peculiar Pippy

Pippy,
This pandemonious dog makes a spiky purr
She expects she is a cat
People stare in confusion.

Strangely
She despises dog food
Admires cat food
As it is heavenly.

Uniquely
She still tries to catch her rough tail
Although she thinks she is a cat.

Catastrophically
She has three legs
Because she fell down 138 steps
She errantly and quickly limps
But tries to trot.

Unusually
She keeps her soft, squeaky bone
In her perfectly O-shaped tail
Because it is her most prized possession.

Peculiar
If you go near her bone
She will hiss
Because she is protective.

Katie Deller (10)
Hartwell Primary School, Hartwell

My Enormous (And Peculiar) Moth

Quaintly,
She flaps limply
Against the monstrous,
Fierce wind.

Using the many faces
On her wings,
She expresses her
Many moods.

Peculiarly healthy
Even though
She only drinks Coke.

Being overly-excited
She gobbles
Greedily and selfishly
While eating her pleasant food.

A crowd-pleasing colossal moth
Grinning gleefully
From the charming attention.

A giant, inspiring moth
With a warm heart
Will help any soul
Without thinking.

Delicately and clumsily
She hovers in the air,
Lopsided.

Pixie Czerniecki (10)
Hartwell Primary School, Hartwell

Omlet The Peculiar Hamster

Omlet
(Who is my pet hamster)
Is very strange.

Oddly,
He roly-polies
In his food bowl,
He is extremely odd.

Omlet
(Who is very unpredictable)
Is always doing new things.

He weirdly adores rabbit food
Which is strange for a hamster.

Omlet
Is always hungry,
He viciously scrabbles unusual food.

Creepily
He stares at you
With his furious face.

Omlet
Rapidly walks sideways
(With a grin),
It's very peculiar!

He looks crazy,
His grey, white fur sticks up.

Illy Wootton (10)
Hartwell Primary School, Hartwell

My Peculiar Fish

Fiercely,
He growls meanly;
He stares with burning red eyes.

Strangely,
His razor-sharp teeth
Can saw through big pieces of meat;
They're pure white.

He's terribly frightening;
You would want to stay away,
Otherwise he'll eat you in one bite.

Oddly,
He keeps his enemies in a castle;
It is always dripping with blood.

He is peculiar.
He only eats digestives and fish.

He is super picky;
He gets his digestives
And his fish from other fish.

Jonathan Bark (10)
Hartwell Primary School, Hartwell

My Peculiar Bunny

Whitey is one of a kind
She has a unique blue
And a dainty green eye.

Unpredictably
She is strange
Only eats nasty donkey legs.

When she dances
Beautifully
She is extremely graceful.

She is deafening
And violently
My ears bleed.

Her squeak is like a horse's neigh
Her voice is cracked
Her throat is sore.

She welcomes people in her territory
When she is feeling extraordinary.

Jessie Barby (10)
Hartwell Primary School, Hartwell

Toby The Peculiar Cat

The midnight-black fur,
Colour changes,
Grey when stroked.

He has lime-green eyes,
He would use them
For staring at animals.

Toby has strong paws
For stamping on his toys roughly.

His greedy meow
Especially for tuna and prawns,
He adores it.

Every morning
He quickly limps
Upstairs into a room.

Unexpectedly,
Toby hates his small litter tray.

Toby admires
Staying inside,
As it's lovely warmth for him.

Jessica Ball (10)
Hartwell Primary School, Hartwell

My Peculiar Cat, Lois

Terribly awkward
Very secretive
Often silent.

She is starving
Loathes cat food
Admires dog food.

Thinks she's a dog
Nibbles and nibbles
Until it's gone.

She is strange
A slight limp
Always tripping.

Despises being alone
Stalks her owner
Around the forest.

Sneakily trails behind
Owner is clueless
Hides cunningly.

Brain muddling
Barks and purrs
Growls at intruders.

Amy Jewell (9)
Hartwell Primary School, Hartwell

Peculiar Pippin

Peculiar Pippin,
Is swifter than Kit, my cat.
Usually a cat
Would be faster than a dog.

Pippin would devour
The weirdest food for a dog
These include grass, onion, carrot and pears
And no other dog eats these foods.

Pippin can play tag,
We didn't teach her,
She would just do it.

Pippin is a border collie.
Border collies round up sheep
But Pippin hates sheep
Because they end up rounding her up!

Zac Gopole (9)
Hartwell Primary School, Hartwell

My Peculiar Pet Fish

He is self-defensive,
Abnormally territorial
And irritably lugubrious.

His black hole mouth is easily triggered,
He inhales aggressively
Then the surroundings are nothing but dust.

He is dreadfully strange,
He has eye-catching lights on his tail,
His elaborate tail illuminates the gloomy water,
Uncontrollably it creates a warning

To ward off predators,
Though there aren't many.
He grows vindictively.

Emma Banham-Hall (9)
Hartwell Primary School, Hartwell

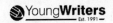

Poppy's Peculiar Pet Hamster

Abnormally,
She is bold,
She believes she is tall
Like a menacing lion.

Millie is very brave
And extremely strange,
She adores performing
And despises keeping still.

Obsessively, she glides
Like an aeroplane,
She lands
On a soft surface.

Like a monkey
She scampers
Determinedly
Up her cage.

She has poor vision
From old age
But mistakes fingers for food.

Poppy Porter (10)

Hartwell Primary School, Hartwell

My Peculiar Dog

Uniquely,
She dances on two paws.
Depressingly,
People stare open-mouthed.

Quickly,
She loathes dog food.
She only eats sensational Birds Eye chicken
burgers
(Which she is obsessed with).

Greedily,
She sucks her burger
Desperate to try the new flavour.

Strangely,
She viciously kills anything that comes near her.
She is extremely territorial.
When someone comes she meows viciously.

Issy Bevan (10)
Hartwell Primary School, Hartwell

Jazz The Peculiar Tortoise

Uniquely
She is ear-splitting
Always wants to play fetch.

Jazz
Ferociously hisses
If needs help
(Like standing up).

She is cute
A well-kept newborn.

Slowly
She rocks in hands
Don't touch if hands are mucky.

Jazz is chirpy
Makes owners' smile.

She always thrilled
In her cage.

Unless it's carrots
She doesn't eat or drink a lot.

Kayce Bridge (10)
Hartwell Primary School, Hartwell

Murphy My Mysterious And Peculiar Cat

Murphy
Who has problems
Growls instead of meowing.

Murphy
Will growl
To scare all away.

As if he's an alien
Every stroke
His hair colour changes.

At any moment
He could be blended into the wall
Ready to pounce.

Murphy
Is annoyingly picky
He only eats biscuits.

You cannot have a biscuit
Within a 10-mile radius
Or Murphy will eat it.

Blake Burton (10)
Hartwell Primary School, Hartwell

My Peculiar Cat

He loathes cat food
But adores tuna and beans
(He believes it tastes heavenly).

Colin
Greedily gobbles his food
Strangely
He admires food more than anything.

Colin enjoys
Wearing hats
He believes they are comfy.

He is very unique
He has 20cm ears
And no tail.

Colin has
Sharp knife-like whiskers
Used to attack enemies.

Daniel Critchley (10)
Hartwell Primary School, Hartwell

My Peculiar Turtle

Timmy
Is peculiar,
He uses armbands,
He can't swim!

In one big gulp
He gobbles his mackerel
Greedily.

He tries to get his own way,
He scowls
And screams
Aggressively.

Annoyingly
His brother teases him
To get attention,
He noisily splashes.

Attractively,
His sequins shine,
Like a diamond.

Georgia Ball (10)
Hartwell Primary School, Hartwell

My Catastrophic And Peculiar Cat

Starsky,
Believes he is the best,
He parades throughout his territory,
Arrogantly.

Unfortunately,
He wondrously imagines
That he doesn't have to follow
Crucial commands.

He is eternally ravishing,
He whacks his brother,
Causing a short argument,
Childishly.

When he becomes annoyed,
Ferociously
He claws.

Abigail Sharp (10)
Hartwell Primary School, Hartwell

My Peculiar Bunny

Uniquely
She is strange
With her mysterious robotic head.

Dolly
That is an adorable robotic rabbit
Can only see out a bit of her beautiful eye.

Although she can still see
She is still a joyful happy rabbit.

She may be sweet
But has always greedily hunted for food.

She may be playful
But is certainly lazy.

Mia-Rose Wilson (10)
Hartwell Primary School, Hartwell

My Peculiar Pet Dog

Walks funny
Thinks he is a celebrity.

He acts really strange
He adores trotting glamourously.

The adorable dog runs quickly
In the lush green garden with delight.

When the furious dog is mad, he bites
Crazily he keeps nipping delicious feet.

Elena Thompson (10)
Hartwell Primary School, Hartwell

My Uniquely Peculiar Dog

Uniquely wired
He dreads dog food
But craves cat food.

His eyes light up glamorously
When he sees a ball of string.

When he's overexcited
He confusingly wags his tail up and down.

Friendly
Welcomes with a cheerful bark.

Alice Hosey (10)
Hartwell Primary School, Hartwell

Mysterious Milo, My Peculiar Dog

Milo,
Unusually is strange,
Urgently loathes the human species.

Uniquely,
He's not gentle (mostly aggressive),
As he had an unwanted past.

He reluctantly snaps,
Only if you try to soothe him,
As he has anger issues.

Skye Peers (10)
Hartwell Primary School, Hartwell

Quinn The Quokkaclown

Q uinn is a quokka and she is a clown.
U nique and untamed she is a circus expert.
I n the circus ring she is amazing.
N ight and day she is always performing.
N ot great at riding a unicycle.

T he best at juggling and gymnastics.
H er life is great, living the circus life.
E veryone buys a ticket to see her.

Q uinn is seven years old and she is a professional.
U nable to do one trick, that is the unicycle.
O n the TV live from the circus, she is famous.
K nown around the whole wide world.
K nown for her special talents, always and forever.
A ustralia is her home and she loves it so much.

Kaycie Comrie (11)
Milesmark Primary School, Rumblingwell

My Pet, Fuddle

When I was five I got a big surprise,
Out between the curtains appeared some eyes,
When I took it in the house
It was as small as a mouse,
But one week later,
It was the size of an alligator!
It is one third pig
And it wears a wig.
It is also one third human
And I think it's a woman.
The rest of it is a fly
But it cannot even fly.
I take her on walks every day,
But she tries to escape in every way!
When she finds a fat spider,
Her belly ends up getting wider,
She used to not be terribly fat
But recently she ate a man called Pat!
But overall she is kind
And she has a caring mind,

Even when she jumps in muddy puddles,
I give Fuddle lots of cuddles.

Finlay Rees (11)

Milesmark Primary School, Rumblingwell

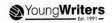
Kindest Not Killer

King is the kindest whale in the ocean
Because he has lots of devotion.
His nickname is the ocean vulture,
Hunting for dead things is part of his culture.
He doesn't believe in the killer whale way,
Killing lots of innocent things every day,
Even though it can be hard,
He killed something once and is forever scarred.
He hates that humans call his friends killers,
Because humans kill all the time for their dinners.
King the kindest whale in the ocean
Is currently working on a potion
So that killer whales don't need to kill anymore,
And so that King's friends don't think being
vegetarian is a bore!

India Wilmshurst (11)
Milesmark Primary School, Rumblingwell

Queenie, Ruler Of All Quolls

Q ueenie is the ruler of all quoll kind.

U pbeat and with very small feet.

E very night she wakes up in a good mood.

E agle-eyed in the dark.

N ight-time is when on quests she'll embark.

I n Australia is where she lives.

E xtroverted she is, always chatting.

T iny little feet patting on the floor.

H er crown always shines.

E ven though she is tiny

Q ueenie can do many things.

U nknown by humans.

O ver time, Queenie has learned to like

L ots of human objects.

L ike cars, bikes, mirrors and many more.

Jessica Thomson (11)

Milesmark Primary School, Rumblingwell

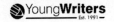
The Very Scary Terry

Hey it's Terry and I was coming to say
It's my right to be scary
And make you feel blue,
It's just what I do.
So this is a warning,
If you think my story is not worth your glory,
Stay away at all costs
And maybe you'll survive another day.
I live in the muck and sometimes I get stuck
Because the coral is very pretty and attractive
And sometimes it pulls me in
And it makes a racket
And fish like to hit me with a hatchet.
I may be big and scary but when it comes to
chasing small fish
I'd rather actually be singing like a canary.

Joseph McDermott (9)
Milesmark Primary School, Rumblingwell

Beware Of Buddy

My name is Buddy, I am a chamelecat.
You may have never heard of me,
That's because I stay hidden in a tree.
I know why I am called a chamelecat,
It's because of my pointy ears,
And my scaly skin.
I've got six thin, wiry whiskers
And a long, furry, wiggly tail.

There is one thing I forgot to mention,
You should never come near enough to bother me,
As my back is loaded with fire infusion,
And if anyone were to threaten me ever,
No one would return to tell the story
And your skeleton would lie in the forest forever.

Phoebe Ward (12)
Milesmark Primary School, Rumblingwell

Marvellous Aros

A rachnophobia is what Aros has.
R idiculously he runs around the house.
O ddly how he eats his food.
S itting on the couch looking at the fat pigeon out the window.

T ickly feet he has.
H owling when he gets left alone.
E veryone loves when he chases his tail.

G rowling when his sister eats his food.
R unning around the garden madly.
E ating lots of treats.
A t breakfast time he likes to bring his cow along.
T o be Aros' owner is such a delight.

Imogen Douglas (11)
Milesmark Primary School, Rumblingwell

Sarah The Superhero

Sarah the superhero is a starfish.
She flies around the world healing the weak and poor.
Off she goes to China to help a pal out.
She meets a girl called Cora
Who is in hospital with a broken nose.
Flick, flick, flick, goes her hand,
Now she's magically healed.
"See you next time," said Sarah
As she's off to help another friend in need.
Oh, she got a call or two or three or twenty.
Gosh, it was a busy day!
Sarah is tired, she went to bed
And had a nice little sleep.
Until tomorrow her work is done!

Imogen Richmond (10)
Milesmark Primary School, Rumblingwell

Everyone Loves Jeb

J ust believe me when I say
E very day is an adventure
B ut when you see Jeb everything is much better.

T he best things about Jeb are
H e has dragon wings and the head of a bear.
E very day is better when you're with Jeb.

S o when you see Jeb, give him a pat or a treat.
H e's not very picky and he likes to make a mess.
E veryone loves Jeb, so go say hi.
E ven a look at his rainbow fur will make your day.
P eople love Jeb, hip hip hooray!

Nieve Taylor (11)
Milesmark Primary School, Rumblingwell

Carla The Caring Cow

Carla the cow took a walk one day
Over the bridges and far away.
An alarm went off from her big blue bow,
With a moo up she went,
She cried, "Oh no!
Someone needs food,
I have something good."
She flew away to Wales
And stopped by a train's rails.
She met a girl called Sam,
"Here you go, have some jam."
With her magic bow she whipped up a house,
Along with it came a pet mouse.
"Thank you so much," said Sam
And off she went in her house full of jam.

Hajra Razzaq (10)
Milesmark Primary School, Rumblingwell

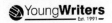

My Pet, Flare

I have a pet called Flare,
She breathes fire and flies through the air.
She has pointy red devil horns,
She's more mystical than unicorns.
She has ruby-red sparkling eyes
And her pointy claws are a magnificent size.
When she's hungry she likes to hunt,
It gives her a sense of amusement.
Her favourite food is goats,
She usually starts at the throat,
She chews its flesh when it's fresh.
I lure her into bed with a big fat chip
Then she'll lie down and have a little kip.

Lola Wilmshurst (11)
Milesmark Primary School, Rumblingwell

Remi The Ray

This is Remi the ray, he is grey.
He doesn't like the ocean,
He much prefers sand,
That's why you see him walking on his hands.
Remi is lazy, grumpy and moody,
He has a big interest in his beauty.
He follows all the latest fashion trends
And doesn't care much about his friends.
He acts brave and strong
But if you think that you are wrong.
Inside he is a soft ray wanting to be loved,
Day after day, week after week.
To everyone: be kind and keep this in mind.

Caitlyn Todman (12)

Milesmark Primary School, Rumblingwell

Rocky Cliffs

R ocky is an earth kind of dragon.

O wning him is quite stressful.

C liffs is his second name.

K indness and passion is his favourite.

Y ou would probably love him.

C leaning him is hard, he always jumps about.

L imes are his favourite food.

I can't wait to watch him grow.

F inding him in hide-and-seek is extremely difficult.

F ury is his best friend.

S o very gentle he sleeps on my lap.

Jack Fraser (10)

Milesmark Primary School, Rumblingwell

Peng The Peculiar Penguin

Let's talk about Peng today,
He's a penguin who likes to play.
On his skateboard for hours on end,
Peng is my best friend.

Black and white colours his coat,
In the water it helps him float.
Having his scarf on day after day,
On the snow he likes to lay.

Kind, cool and fluffy,
Tiny, cute and messy.
Those are the words to describe him.
He likes a lot of things but not the gym.

Lewis Greig (11)
Milesmark Primary School, Rumblingwell

Big Blue The Big Bullfrog

Big Blue loves his lake,
His lake is very big and blue.
He loves to go croak, croak,
To let me know he wants food.
He loves to eat his beloved mealworms.
All day he'll lay in the sun,
I sometimes join him for a swim,
Then I go back to the reeds,
The reeds are where I watch him from.
Then at night he goes to bed
To have some rest
Then I feed him his mealworms
Then I go for another swim.

Emma Arnold (10)
Milesmark Primary School, Rumblingwell

Connie The Cow

C aring, loveable cow she is.

O n the pitch doing cheerleading.

N ever will be mean to you.

N obody will be left out when you're with Connie.

I n her room, getting a fashionable outfit.

E very day she makes millions.

C onnie will always have your back.

O n the go to her cheerleading practice.

W hen you're by her side you will feel safe.

Madeline Asher (11)
Milesmark Primary School, Rumblingwell

Griffiphant

G arry is so cool.

R eally he is.

I f you think by cool it means he sits in a pool

F or your information, it's not what you think it is.

F unny and serious.

I t's quite extraordinary.

P eople should be afraid.

H as a griffin body

A nd an elephant trunk.

N early an eagle.

T he only griffiphant is Garry.

Joseph Whyte (12)

Milesmark Primary School, Rumblingwell

Max The Magic

M y life is marvellous.
A ll I like to eat is bananas.
X mas is my favourite time of year.

T he jungle is the best.
H appy Easter.
E aster is nice.

M y house is messy.
A lovely monkey I am.
G in I like to drink.
I n my house it's just amazing.
C an I have a banana?

Struan Henderson (9)
Milesmark Primary School, Rumblingwell

Secret Agent Giraffe

Secret Agent Giraffe
Running along the path
Looking for dangerous crimes
In a really quick time
Down in an alleyway in Cannes
Following a suspicious man
With a gun in his hand
Talking about an underground plan
That is taking place later
Holding a piece of paper
In his hands that looks like a map
Of a woman's house called Pat.

Dylan Federico Ashe (10)
Milesmark Primary School, Rumblingwell

DJ Tiko

T he best DJ alive.
I n the world no one better.
K indness nowhere near him
O r be his friend.

F or a start there's a world record.
I s there better? No there's not!
S top being silly, try him now.
H ow will you lose because you are bad.
Y ou better watch out, here he comes!

Kerr Kelso (8)
Milesmark Primary School, Rumblingwell

Bob The Bold Cat

B ob is not usually friendly.
O dd because Bob jumps out of aeroplanes.
B est at being crazy.

B ad at not being crazy.
O nly good at being sassy.
L oud and sometimes annoying.
D odges water.

C ourageous sometimes.
A nd hates cat food.
T errifying sometimes.

Connor Henderson (8)
Milesmark Primary School, Rumblingwell

Harry Hippo

Harry is a hippo, he wants to climb a tree
But when he gets there he thinks he needs a pee.
He goes to a lake to do a pee,
Oh no! He gets attacked by a snake!
Harry runs but the snake is fast
And Harry finally outruns the snake at last.
Harry is tired.
He was never agile
So it's time to rest for a while.

Jack Rees (9)

Milesmark Primary School, Rumblingwell

Wildtim Bunny

W eird.

I ntelligent.

L oves carrots.

D oes poops on random people.

T ricky to feed.

I ntimidating.

M agical power.

B en's popular pet.

U nsad.

N o avocados.

N o celery.

Y ou will be saved if in danger.

Benjamin Fraser (8)

Milesmark Primary School, Rumblingwell

Super Pig

S aturn flying Superman.

U p and down again and again.

P ie is his favourite food.

E lla is his pig girlfriend.

R uaridh is his superhero best friend.

P ig. The pig is grumpy.

I 'm a caveman in the jungle.

G ood at football.

Jack Heath (8)
Milesmark Primary School, Rumblingwell

Fire Fury

F laming like a torch.
I like him how he is.
R eally clever.
E xtraordinary.

F ind him in my room, he'll be sleeping in my bed.
U nique.
R ide on his back and you'll feel alive.
Y elling 'hello' as we pass by!

Matthew Kay (10)
Milesmark Primary School, Rumblingwell

Super Speedy Sammy Seal

S ammy has super speed.
A bsolutely adorable.
M iraculously smooth.
M arvellously gentle.
Y oghurt is what Sammy loves.

S ammy has a son called Finlay.
E xcitedly playful.
A lfie is his owner.
L iam is his friend.

Alfie Colgan (9)
Milesmark Primary School, Rumblingwell

Rory Raptor

R ory is good at roaring.
O ften eats meat.
R ips clothes.
Y ellow backpack.

R eally fast at running.
A lways hungry.
P ainter of colourful pictures.
T umbles all the time.
O dd.
R apid eater.

Blair Snedker (7)
Milesmark Primary School, Rumblingwell

Poppy The Precious Panda

Poppy, my precious panda
I love to see you above
You're the best one out there
And the only one I love.

Oh how I wish to be one of you
I would do anything to make that come true.

Oh my Poppy, you're so cute
But sometimes I wish you were less mute.

Madison Park (10)
Milesmark Primary School, Rumblingwell

My Fish, Lolly

L olly is a fish.
O nly eats fish and corn.
L ives on land.
L oves going to the club.
Y es, Lolly is the best.

F astest in the world.
I s crazy.
S ometimes Lolly is nice.
H ouse is in the grass.

Abigail Fraser (8)
Milesmark Primary School, Rumblingwell

My Fire Dragon

F laming beast.
I ncredible at night.
R ain fire.
E ndangered.

D angerous at day.
R ages at a fight.
A mazing in lava.
G roans every day.
O dd.
N ice at night.

Jack D'Sylva (9)
Milesmark Primary School, Rumblingwell

The Amazing Lill Piglet

Lill Piglet is not just any pig
'Cause lots of people love her music.
She has got plenty of money.
I know because guess what?
Lill Piglet is my sister.
Even though she is famous
She is there for me when I need her the most.

Leonie Kemp (10)
Milesmark Primary School, Rumblingwell

Jimmy

Jimmy, the juggling deer hippo dog,
Tall and skinny and funny like a log.

J ust like a dog, I look like a log.
I am a loving thing.
M essy I am.
M agic I can do.
Y oghurt is the best.

Liam Arnold (9)
Milesmark Primary School, Rumblingwell

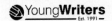

Bob Good Giraffe

B est at being crazy.
O bviously loves gold.
B est at fighting.

G reatest at football.
O bsessed with exercise.
O ddly strong with muscles.
D on't mess with me!

Rylie Smart (8)
Milesmark Primary School, Rumblingwell

Queen Blobby

B eautiful Queen Blobby

L oving life as a queen.

O rdinary is not his thing

B ut being awesome is just right.

B y the end of Blobby's day

Y ou can say he's full of delight.

Jenna Heath (11)
Milesmark Primary School, Rumblingwell

Squirtle The Turtle

S illy Squirtle has a really big body.

Q uite cute.

U nordinary.

I t is special.

R eally adventurous in a good way.

T erritorial.

L ovely.

E nchanted.

Abigail Morton (8)

Milesmark Primary School, Rumblingwell

The Curry Panda

P ut the curry on the table and eat it.

E aster is Perry's favourite celebration.

R eally likes football.

R eally likes curry.

Y ou don't want to smell Perry's farts!

Ben Watson (10)

Milesmark Primary School, Rumblingwell

The Escape From Containment

This is the great escape.
The guards made a grave mistake.
Firing and firing.
They're going to need to do some hiring.
A lizard in a containment room.
They all knew they were doomed!

Coby Thomson (10)
Milesmark Primary School, Rumblingwell

Rocky The Rock Star

R eally good at playing the guitar.
O dd and likes to rock out.
C ould play the piano.
K now that he could be in a concert.
Y ou have to watch out for him.

Maia Harker (8)
Milesmark Primary School, Rumblingwell

Match The Cat

M ostly playing football.
A match.
T hey are all friends, some of them are
C heetahs, but they are all friends. They're
H ighly effective at football.

Munroe Candlish (8)
Milesmark Primary School, Rumblingwell

Superstar Fox

S illy
U nhappy
P layful
E ater
R unner
S leepy
T eleporting
A lways dumpster jumping
R ock star.

Theerathan (8)
Milesmark Primary School, Rumblingwell

Clay The Long Dog

My name is Clay,
I am tame,
I also love to play.
I also like to go on walks,
To go on the bungee.
But I am too long
So I go off into the sky to fly.

Kimberley Matysiak (10)
Milesmark Primary School, Rumblingwell

My Giraffe Called Thing

T his is my giraffe.
H e runs about all over the place.
I like catching him.
N o one knows about it.
G iraffes are cool.

Rory Vaughan (7)

Milesmark Primary School, Rumblingwell

The Bunny's Life

I am in a prison,
In a cell,
I am getting out now
With Gerald the lion.
"Come on Gerald,
We gotta go,
This place is going down!"

Cameron Ritchie (10)
Milesmark Primary School, Rumblingwell

Duggy

D uggy digs mud.
U nder mud he has a house.
G erald is muddy too.
G reat at being messy.
Y ou are always muddy.

Zoe Christie (8)
Milesmark Primary School, Rumblingwell

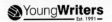

Onyx

O rthocones are massive.
N ot ever this mutated.
Y ou are like an ant to this titan.
X mas freezes me so I swim south.

Iustin Pichiu (9)
Milesmark Primary School, Rumblingwell

Boby Dog

B oby sings.

O n a rock Boby sings.

B oby sings in bed.

Y ellow is Boby's favourite colour.

Katy Arnold (7)

Milesmark Primary School, Rumblingwell

Francis The Flying Frog

F rancis is a frog

R eally small with huge blue eyes

A weird frog Francis is

N ot because of his big eyes or ginger Afro

'C ause he has golden chicken wings to fly through the night

I t's very strange, I know

S ome frogs are jealous whilst some admire

T he amazing beauty before their eyes

H e struts around in his pink heels

E veryone adores him.

F lying through the night sky

L ying down in the day

Y odeling in the afternoon

I don't know how the other frogs cope!

N apping is his hobby

G liding through the sky is his fav!

F abulous Francis the frog
R oaming the town
O wning the place
G lorious Francis the frog!

Sienna Pike (9)

Millbrook Community Primary School, Kirkby

The Monkey Who Robbed A Bank

B ad monkey, go to bed!

A mazing, now he's asleep, I'm going too.

D ay came. Mason awoke from his deep sleep.

"M ason, what do you want for breakfast?" "Nothing," he shouted.

O ff he went in a click of a finger.

N ow the plan begins... I heard a faint squeaky noise.

K itted out ready for the battle to commence.

E xcitedly I ran after Mason.

"Y ou will never catch me!"

B ank-robbing genius I am. Wait, he didn't stop but the

A crobatic monkey cartwheeled through the guards.

D own he came with a cheeky smile, now that he has got a lot of gold that will last him a while.

Ethan Lundon (10)
Millbrook Community Primary School, Kirkby

174

The Hopping Hamster

H op, hop, hop, here he comes, he is so small.

O nly if he was bigger but he doesn't like that idea.

P onds are dangerous.

P uddles are too.

I ndividual, the only one is him.

N om, nom, nom, he just ate a crumb, now he is full.

G reeting you just there, 3cm tall, jumping on his toes.

H amsters are already small, he is that times two.

A n unusual size and unusual speed, he jumps.

M aximum speed and jump.

S tep by step he'll beat you.

T alking mean to him.

E ntering everything.

R un, run, run!

Riley B V (9)

Millbrook Community Primary School, Kirkby

The Flying Sloth

S lothacorn is not your ordinary pet.

L ots of people wouldn't come up with this pet.

O ther people may say it's weird, but in my vision it's perfect.

T he other animals wouldn't expect this pet.

H ere it is with all its magic.

A n animal you can never underestimate

'C ause it may be mean but it's an angel really!

O f course it likes to dance and prance in the sky.

R ight after it starts to dance it goes to sleep in a second.

N ow, could you underestimate Slothacorn?

Ruby Lynskey (9)
Millbrook Community Primary School, Kirkby

Angel Fox

A n angel fox is a fox with a halo and wings.

N o other animal looks like this.

G reat animals are good but this cheeky one isn't.

E veryone wants this pet because of how legendary it is.

L egendary animals you can find but some can't.

F inding this pet will be really impossible.

O ther pets can be nice and mean but my animal is both.

e **X** actly loads of pets can be weird but mine is way weirder.

Annie-Mai Brown (9)

Millbrook Community Primary School, Kirkby

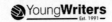

The Shark In The Suit

I have a pet, I named it Jerold,
It's a peculiar pet to say the least.
Every time I look he's gone somewhere
To do an agent mission.
I found him in a building fighting a whole army of men.
He's faster than a shooting star,
He doesn't need a special agent car.
He fights better than a warrior,
He couldn't feel sorrier.
He jumps 200ft high
Without a try.
Jerold is his name,
I guess a special agent shark is handy.

Jacob Fisher (10)
Millbrook Community Primary School, Kirkby

Dino Dog

I went to a dog shelter,
There were many dogs and puppies
But one looked rather odd.
The owners told me she was a beagle
So I decided to adopt her.
She acted like a normal dog
But one night I heard a very loud bang.
I went downstairs to check what happened
And there was a dinosaur in my house!
I panicked until I realised
That Dino was my dog!
She may be weird or odd
But she is my dino dog!

Elizabeth Lewis (10)

Millbrook Community Primary School, Kirkby

Dave The Distinctive Duck

Dave is a duck,
An unusual duck,
A glow-in-the-dark duck,
A go-to-the-park duck,
A riding-a-bike duck,
A going-on-a-hike duck,
A flying-to-the-moon duck,
On-top-of-a-balloon duck,
A reading-a-book duck,
A Gordon Ramsay-cook duck.
So, as you can see,
Dave is no ordinary duck,
In fact, I think
Dave is a super duck!

Annie Browne (10)
Millbrook Community Primary School, Kirkby

Dino Cat

D ino Cat is very special.
I t lives in Japan.
N o one has ever seen it,
O r if they have seen it, it roars.

C ats are cool but Dino Cat is better.
A little bit of trouble you can get into with Dino Cat.
T o get help say, "Dino Cat!"

Jasmine Jones (9)
Millbrook Community Primary School, Kirkby

YoungWriters Est. 1991

Super Dog

S uperhero is my dog.
U tterly incredible.
P erfect in every way.
E xtraordinary and smart.
R unning as fast as he can.

D og is really a cat.
O MG is this true?
G rumpy he never is.

Andrew James (10)
Millbrook Community Primary School, Kirkby

The Tech Pup 2000

T he tech pup 2000 is my special pup.
A dorable as any dog at the vet.
R uns faster than a car, grabs a drink and says,
"Taa!"
A stonishing as anything.

Lewis Doran (10)

Millbrook Community Primary School, Kirkby

Coolastic Karl

C oolastic Karl is an extraordinary pet.

O n Mondays we like to stretch.

O n Fridays we like to relax.

L and hole! Golfing is where our friendship began.

A nd Karl loves to build.

S tretch, stretch!

T ime to go to the playground.

I n a gym, exercising is amazing!

C oconut pie is cool, Karl's favourite.

K arl is smelling the yummy pie

A nd it looks like heaven's pie!

R eally stretching to get that milk.

L arge and cute is my best friend, Karl.

Yue Yang (9)
Millbrook School, Cheshunt

My Cool Little Bunny

R ock Star is a bunny that is scary, it can scare with a furious lion roar!

O nly I can have it because the world only has one.

C an she rock? Oh yes she can!

K ind little bunny.

S tarts to rock to the night sky like dynamite.

T onight we are going to eat roast meat

A nd sleep tight my little bunny. Tomorrow we are going to...

R ock to the beat!

Laura Yu (9)
Millbrook School, Cheshunt

Rocky The Cat

Rocky flew as fast as an aeroplane in the sky.
He held up his trusty guitar high up
And said, "Are you ready?"
On stage then he started a song,
That was as loud as a dino's roar.
The crowd cheered
And threw flowers as he continued.
By the time we went home
A whole crowd followed us,
It was truly an amazing day.

Arjed Brooks-Taberos (9)
Millbrook School, Cheshunt

My Magic Monkey Show

M y mysterious monkey.
A mazing magic.
G entle rabbit in the hat.
I mpressive magic tricks.
C ute monkey.

M arvellous show.
O dd bananas.
N ew magic.
K indly dangerous.
E xtraordinary show.
Y ummy bananas.

Kara Williams (9)
Millbrook School, Cheshunt

Oreocorn

O reocorn is a cute pet.

R eally good at ice skating.

E ats peanuts, nuts and cornflakes.

O reo is the smartest because he can ice skate.

C ute as a strawberry.

O reocorn is a special pet.

R eally kind and pretty.

N ever bites people.

Zuzanna Michalowska (9)

Millbrook School, Cheshunt

Cëchófz

C ëchófz is a troublemaker.

Ë xtraordinary and deadly.

C ome and see the monstrosity.

H ilarious when they juggle apples.

Ó h you can't see them!

F amous for juggling in circuses.

Z oo it should be in.

Lydia Toms (8)
Millbrook School, Cheshunt

Snowball

S nowball is very clever.

N ever do you listen.

O h naughty you are.

W ater drips from the straw.

B ut I love your handstands.

A nd how cute you look.

L ook at your messy house.

L ove Snowball, goodnight.

Poppy-Rose Irons (9)

Millbrook School, Cheshunt

Sapphire The Bunny

S assy as can be.

A mazing like a star.

P retty as a princess.

P op! Bang! This bunny is perfection.

H ungry like always.

I rresistible like a sweet.

R eady to talk to you.

E ager to talk as always.

Tara Brown-Anderson (9)
Millbrook School, Cheshunt

Fluffy The Dogo

F luffy as a cloud.
L ightning fast.
U tterly cute.
F un.
F antastic.
Y oung at heart.

D ashes through the park.
O bedient.
G entle.
O ozing with love.

Rubie Crouch (9)
Millbrook School, Cheshunt

Teddy

T eddy is as fun as a ball and he likes his treats.
E asy Teddy you are crazy like a bear!
D id you eat your dinner you crazy dog?
D id you have a good fly you munchkin?
Y ou are a lazy, crazy munchkin?

Fletcher Killingback (8)
Millbrook School, Cheshunt

Cherry

Me and my pet dog, Cherry are in the garden
playing.
When I go to sleep he goes to sneak.
He goes in the clouds and flies around
And it is fun and he messes around.
He goes hip hip hooray all around town.

Naomi Igboanusi (9)
Millbrook School, Cheshunt

Myloof

M yloof is a cute dog.
Y ou can bark like a trumpet.
L ovely and gentle.
O h, you ate my chips
O n my floor.
F unny earrings are amazing.

Dempsey Wilson (9)
Millbrook School, Cheshunt

Super Frix

Me and my pet rabbit called Frix went for a walk.
I let him run around
Then he found a cute cape.
He put it on
And started to fly with a zoom.

Joao Antonio Almeida (8)
Millbrook School, Cheshunt

Dumbo The Elephant

D angerously cute.

U seful for flying.

M arvellous magic elephant.

B ravely bold.

O beying their owner.

Aidan Paterson (8)

Millbrook School, Cheshunt

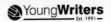

Nina

N ot afraid.

I ncredible speed.

N ice.

A lways acrobatic.

Kyle Craig (9)

Millbrook School, Cheshunt

David Grylls

David Grylls is a hairy beast.
He likes to feast.
With his long beard he is unbeatable.
He's better than Sky Brown.

He does an ollie that sends him into space.
He is a longboard ace.
But he landed on his face.
Sometimes his longboard catches on fire.
Luckily that makes him zoom even higher.

Sky Brown says she would be the youngest
Olympic competitor
But David Grylls has already competed and he's by
far the hairiest!

Alex Sawyer (10)
Ravensden CE Primary Academy, Ravensden

Beware Brown Bear

Beware of the skateboarding bear,
He has frizzy hair!
If you sit in his chair
You will be crying in despair.
He is full of scare
And he's a millionaire!
He is as brown as a muffin,
Well that's his name,
Along with his golden chain.

Muffin likes to skate,
He is really is great.
He is that awesome you can't debate.
He also fights, it's kind of right.
Muffin is just my peculiar pet.

Summer Upshaw (11)
Ravensden CE Primary Academy, Ravensden

My Pet, Rocky

My favourite pet is called Rocky
But some people think he's a little cocky.
Rocky is a Steller sea lion
That has a brother called Bryan.
His favourite colour is purple
And he likes to hang around with his friend, Turtle
Who likes to jump over hurdles.
He loves to swim
But sometimes it hurts his limbs.
He also likes to skate
But he would really rather bake.
Rocky road is his favourite thing to make.

Ella Southam (11)
Ravensden CE Primary Academy, Ravensden

The Daring Dugong Darrel

The daring Dugong Darrel,
As evil as can be,
Shape-shifting's one of his powers,
He can turn into a bunch of flowers,
He uses his powers for bad,
He makes the world go mad,
His tail is a bumpy road,
Flying's another power of his,
He zooms through the air with a whizz,
Never go near my pet
Or pain will be the best that you get.

Leo Bell (9)
Ravensden CE Primary Academy, Ravensden

Steller The Surfing Sea Lion

My pet sea lion, Steller
Thinks that she's the smartest
But every single day
I see her ride the waves.

Little old Steller is good
At riding waves.
She's better than Sky Brown
Always every day.

Boom! Crash! Bang!
I saw the waves get higher.
Steller didn't mind
Because she's a brave sea lion.

Zachary Dunn (9)
Ravensden CE Primary Academy, Ravensden

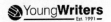

My Dugong

My dugong lives in the sea
And its closest cousin is a manatee.

It lives in shallow waters
And it has some daughters.

My dugong is grey
And it likes to play
And his name is Jay.

He's almost completely a herbivore
And his core is as strong as Thor.

Ethan Richard Murgatroyd (10)
Ravensden CE Primary Academy, Ravensden

My Dugong

He's like a beautiful butterfly gliding through the water.
Rather lazy, never very active.
Smarter than you, never as can be.
As gentle as a giant and tame forever.
Never hurts a soul.
His powers are amazing.
He helps the ocean not to die from human life.

Jacob Shufflebotham (11)
Ravensden CE Primary Academy, Ravensden

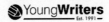

Stella

Stella is a supersonic seal
That can't slow down
Stella loves volleyball
Because she always wins
Using her flippers and tail
To slow the ball into the soft sand.

Valentino Alessi (11)

Ravensden CE Primary Academy, Ravensden

Sophie At The Aquarium

Every time I go to the aquarium
I see Sophie swimming all over.
I can't keep her at home,
She's too big!
I love her though,
My Steller sea lion!

Paige Davenport (10)
Ravensden CE Primary Academy, Ravensden

Machiavellian Mereoleona

There are many abnormal furry companions out there, but,

There is one that you won't assume that they're a pet.

She has lustful sapphire eyes that scintillate more than fireworks.

She has lengthy, wavy, vermillion-coloured hair (including horns).

She has majestic crimson-coloured markings around her breathtaking eyes. She has ginormous serrated teeth that look sharper than a chainsaw!

Mereoleona has long scaly horns.

As well as a sign that removes demonic spirits.

Mereoleona possesses a fluffy tail at first.

Until there's a gradient leading to a thin squamous tail.

Mereoleona is an anomalous creature.

From what I've been trying to point out,

Multiple people will be thinking that she may be a partly furry crocodile that possesses magical powers or something.

Whatever you said is probably wrong.
Concluding everything I said, Mereoleona is a...

Gabriella Peters (11)

St Bridget's Primary RC School, Baillieston

The Fox In The Box!

One strange night I found a box,
Inside it was a massive fox!
Beside him lay a black top hat,
A magic wand lay next to that.
He said he could perform multiple tricks,
But the effects could not be fixed.
So out he got and waved his wand,
And took me to a magical pond!
"But I can't swim!" I said in fear,
Then he said, "Now you can, my dear!"
He tapped me with his magic stick,
And it all happened very quick.
Before I knew it I could swim,
In a pond that was filled to the brim.
But this pond was very weird, next thing I knew,
I had a beard!
"What have you done, you cheeky fox!
You should just go back into your box!"
I took him home to be my pet,
In the hope that my wonderful wish will be met,

To not have this beard,
That makes me look weird.

Paige Logan (11)

St Bridget's Primary RC School, Baillieston

Speedy The Snail

This is Speedy the snail,
The snail who is quite strange.
This is what she's been born with,
The problem will never change.

She speeds across the garden,
But she always comes back clean.
Compared to the dog at home,
She's always like the *Queen!*

When she looks at the dog,
She can see that he could leap.
Every time she tries to,
She always falls asleep!

Zoe Shek (12)
St Bridget's Primary RC School, Baillieston

Sneaky Cheeky

Every night once I'm asleep,
A fox comes out and sits on my street.
I named him Cheeky,
Because he's very sneaky.

He loves to play with toys,
But he never makes a noise!
He looks very freaky,
And his voice is quite squeaky.

He is a bit small,
And has hardly any hair at all.
His eyes are dark as coal,
And you can see right into his soul.

Ciara Tracy (11)
St Bridget's Primary RC School, Baillieston

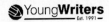

Crocodog

There once was a dog called Crocodog,
Who loved to play with other dogs.
In less than a minute
He'd reached his limit,
And *snapped* within his great big jaws.
If you go near him,
Next time you'll fear him
As he strikes with his great big claws!

Andrew Provan (12)
St Bridget's Primary RC School, Baillieston

Finn The Fish Dog

Running through the park,
Going on a walk.
Playing in the garage
Chewing on your socks.

Here comes Finn,
Rising out the water.
Chasing the dogs,
Now he's getting hotter.

Ava Curran (12)

St Bridget's Primary RC School, Baillieston

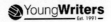

Juggler Joe

There once was a snail named Joe
Who was like all snails, very slow
But he enjoyed to juggle
Then started to struggle
So he ordered two hot dogs to go!

Sophia Smith (12)
St Bridget's Primary RC School, Baillieston

The Adventures Of Bradley Star

B radley is an extremely handsome hamster, saving lives with his incredible eyes.

R iding in to get some fame, showing off with no shame.

A ppreciate his moves, he's saving lives as he does.

D ancing, partying all night long, listening to his favourite song.

L ucas, his amazing partner, supporting him all the way.

E ver thought the job is dangerous? Bradley is determined to stay.

Y ou may think he is nice, well you might want to think twice.

S ome think he is too good to be true.

T he tale of the amazing pet

A ngry at Bradley's power, hungry to seek it for themselves.

R arely you might see his face and if you don't believe it, you are a disgrace.

Lucas Freeman (9)

St Mary's Hampton CE Primary School, Hampton

Sensational Stingray

There he was,
Sensational Stingray, fighting criminals once again.
He was fighting bad baboon.
It was a close fight,
But Sensational Stingray won again.
He won thanks to his super stinger,
Flying skills and
His fire-breathing skills.

Suddenly,
Sensational Stingray heard something
Boom!
It was the Danger Gang
(Terrifying Tiger, Scary Snake, Hyper Hyena,
Petrifying Panther and Eerie Eagle).
They were there,
To fight Sensational Stingray.
The fight was about to begin.

The Danger Gang vs Sensational Stingray.
Sensational Stingray put his invisibility cloak on.
No one could see him.

Where was he?

All of a sudden,

Sensational Stingray jumped out and stung Hyper Hyena.

That was the end of Hyper Hyena...

All of a sudden, Terrifying Tiger took Sensational Stingray's invisibility cloak.

It was one against four!

Then Scary Snake spat his poison,

But Sensational Stingray dodged.

Sensational Stingray flew

Over the Danger Gang

And threw his cape on Petrifying Panther's eyes.

Petrifying Panther couldn't see anything.

Sensational Stingray had the chance to get Petrifying Panther,

Whilst he couldn't see!

So he stung Petrifying Panther.

That was the end of Petrifying Panther...

It was just three against one!

Who was going to win?

Sensational Stingray or the Danger Gang?

Suddenly, Eerie Eagle flew over
And tried to rip his talons in Sensational Stingray's skin.
Sensational Stingray ducked and Eerie Eagle missed.

Sensational Stingray flew up and so did Eerie Eagle
It was one vs one
In the air.
Eerie Eagle vs Sensational Stingray.
Eerie Eagle dived towards Sensational Stingray
To attack.
Sensational Stingray dodged.
Then he breathed his fire on Eerie Eagle.
Eerie Eagle was gone!

With Eerie Eagle gone
It was Scary Snake and Terrifying Tiger vs Sensational Stingray.
Suddenly Scary Snake coiled around Sensational Stingray.
Sensational Stingray was trapped...
How could he get out?

Then, all of a sudden,
Sensational Stingray turned his stinger on and
Then Scary Snake died.
It was just Sensational Stingray and Terrifying
Tiger left.
Who was going to win?
Out of nowhere,
Terrifying Tiger tried to scratch Sensational
Stingray
But of course,
Sensational Stingray dodged.
Then Sensational Stingray breathed his fire on
Terrifying Tiger,
And that was the end of the Danger Gang.

Pavalan Nursimloo (10)
St Mary's Hampton CE Primary School, Hampton

Posh Bear's Astonishing Day

Posh Bear opened his fridge and, to his surprise,
there was a bottle of champagne lying next to his
fries.
He picked it up and flicked the cork and he called
for his retainer.
He came to his aid and gave him a game to play
for the day.
He drank his champagne.
He went to his room and wore a funny scent
And wrote with his favourite fountain pen.
He wrote an invitation for all of his 27 human-like
friends.
He called his retainer to deliver the letters.
He slicked his hair back and looked like a hare.
He heard a sound, *ding, ding!*
His visitors were here.
Posh Bear opened the door to go out of his room
And saw 25+ of his friends were here in a fancy
suit
But the rest didn't care.

Posh Bear was a really nice guy
And was always fair.
He gave everyone a glass of champagne with the side of a baguette.
Time went by and they were having fun dancing in the ballroom
And talking about a new TV programme that sounded nice.
It was time for everyone to leave.
Posh Bear was sad, really, really sad,
He started to cry next to his bag.
It was time for tea but he couldn't spread his butter because he forgot to give his guests a little present but then he remembered he could send it in a letter.
Posh Bear wasn't the smartest little chap
But he had a big heart.
One day he heard a ding, ding!
His retainer opened the door and he heard a familiar voice
Then he saw his mother in a big dress.
He gave her a hug and he felt really stressed.
He didn't have this planned so he didn't know what to do.

She said one of his friends told her at the candy shop
The letter that he had given her said she had a thousand pounds so in return she helped Posh Bear to spend time with his mother.
He was very, very happy and now his day had got a lot brighter.

Israela Adeyoju (10)
St Mary's Hampton CE Primary School, Hampton

The Yellow Fox

One day as I lay in bed
A yellow fox jumped in my head.
I had to look not once but twice
Because he held a pizza slice.
You will not believe what next I saw...
A sausage roll in his other paw,
Not only did he have those plates,
He was also wearing roller skates!
Just as I thought it could not get more wrong
He played my favourite Boyzone song.
He slowly started counting sheep
And then fell into a deep sleep
As I crept up to take a look
My heartbeat quickened and my fingers shook.
I slowly reached out to touch his fur
When the strangest thing did occur.
He disappeared in a puff of smoke
And just like that, from a dream, I woke.

Poppy Halpin (9)
St Mary's Hampton CE Primary School, Hampton

A Beach Day With Fey

Me and my mercat, Fey
Went out for a day,
At the beach to play.
I got her out of her water tank,
Then got her breathing helmet from my secret
piggy bank.
My mercat, Fey, was half fish you see,
One way or another she needed to breathe!
We packed our bags and hit the road,
While Fey ate cat treats, made of Lego.
This is the only thing she can digest,
Anything else would come back as a mess!
We drove and drove,
Across the road,
Faster and faster to the beach we would go!
We jump out of the car and onto the sand,
Running and running across the dry land.
We jumped into the massive blue,
Fey took off her helmet, it was about time too.
Faster and faster we raced in the sun,
Then we had fish and chips and more ice creams
than one!

We then ran and we ran, across the white sand,
When home time came, we were really quite sad.
We drove until noon,
We could see the full moon.
Me and Fey went to bed,
To rest our sleepy, tired heads.
One thing's for sure, this day wouldn't be the same,
Without the one and the only mercat, Fey.

Lois Luyombya (10)
St Mary's Hampton CE Primary School, Hampton

I Love My Pet

I love my pet, I really do,
But once it chewed through my shoe.
Then before I knew,
My dog grew and grew.
It stood at 50 metres tall,
Which made me feel quite small.
I love my pet, I really do,
But give me a clue,
Why my dog can run faster than you?
500 miles per hour,
Is my dog's superpower.
I love my pet, I really do,
But when it gets excited it turns invisible too,
It hides away,
Until the end of the day.
I love my pet, I really do,
But sometimes it flies away, who knew.
Off it goes, up and away,
Where it goes no one will say.
I love my pet, I know that's true,
I love my pet, I really do.

Aliana Protopapa-Marnoch (10)
St Mary's Hampton CE Primary School, Hampton

Potato The Goat

P otatoes are his favourite food.

O nce he was not allowed to eat potatoes so he was in a mood.

T wo times I've seen him doing opera,

A nd ever since he was little, dreaming to be an orca.

T en times flying on a motorbike

O ne hundred times flying on a motorbike and singing opera with a hairbrush.

T he goat doesn't have a toothbrush.

H e has very dirty teeth.

E leven friends called Keith,

G arry is his BFF.

O ne day doctors proved he was deaf.

A ctually, they proved he was blind.

T hen proved he was out of his mind.

Bibi Roisin Adams (9)

St Mary's Hampton CE Primary School, Hampton

Computer Cat

C an you beat him in a game? No you can't!

O n games that are grindy most of the time.

M ostly plays Roblox but plays Minecraft too.

P lays on the computer all the time.

U nreal Engine and Steam plays as well.

T en trillion hours of playing games.

E xotic food and drink the Computer Cat has.

R oblox is his favourite game.

C an beat you in any game.

A mong Us is one of his favourite games.

T and can't beat him!

Oliver Tattam (10)

St Mary's Hampton CE Primary School, Hampton

The Excellent Elastacat

It all began with one little cat,
One giraffe and a lazy sausage dog.
They were walking down the pavement
When all of a sudden,
A tall man dressed all in black appeared with a machine.
He said that they should get into the machine
And that's how the elastacat was made.
Whoosh! You would hear as we zoomed down the street
On the back of my elastacat, *bang!*
Oh you silly elastacat,
Don't bang into the lamp post.

Amelia Veasey (10)
St Mary's Hampton CE Primary School, Hampton

Tales Of Wrinkleton

Wrinkleton looks scary you see
But he really can be such a charm, also a delight
He can't see well
I guess you could say he lost his sight
He struggled through a lot
A lot he struggled through
He is playful
He is joyful
He really is kind
I hope you want to meet him
He has never been dim
And if you ever see him you might be scared
But don't worry, he won't bite
I mean, he might...

Ivy George (9)
St Mary's Hampton CE Primary School, Hampton

Sleepy Savana

S leepy Savana made her way to the fridge.

A person spotted Savana drooling at the fabulous fridge.

V ases were what the lazy cat loathed. She would break them all the time.

A cat was robbing the cat bank when it was night.

"N asty little cat!" the figure shouted, waking everyone up.

A t Savana's house, her owners would go out for dates every Friday.

Zoe Brown (8)

St Mary's Hampton CE Primary School, Hampton

Gangster Hamster

G angster hamster.
A mazing rapper.
N utella is his favourite food.
G angster
S uper rapper.
T rying to make a teleportation device.
E nergetic hamster.
R ascal.

H ero.
A gile.
M agnificent troop leader.
S uper DJ.
T rillion pounds.
E xcellent gangster
R apper.

India Howard (9)
St Mary's Hampton CE Primary School, Hampton

The Colour Change Bunny

One sunny day I went walking
And I saw the most amazing thing.
I saw a blue bunny.
The bunny started running fast as I walked past.
It was changing colour as it went to its pet store.
I thought, *can I buy the bunny?*
Then I realised my money I'd spent.
Then, when I farted the blue bunny came out
And started to fart
And I made it my funny bunny,
My peculiar pet.

Dilakshika Shanmaganathan (9)

St Mary's Hampton CE Primary School, Hampton

The Black Cat

Once upon a time
The black cat rhymed
He lurked into my room
And said, "Boom!"
I screamed like a bird
And then heard
Every noise was in my head
I forgot about it and went to bed
But something caught my eye
The black cats lie
I went downstairs
I saw a ball bounce by
The black cat's cry
And then he ran
And then I had to sleep in the van.

Sophie McCann (9)
St Mary's Hampton CE Primary School, Hampton

Big Bunny

My bunny likes the beach
And his favourite food is peach.
He doesn't know how to rhyme on time
Or go online
But at least Big Bunny is very funny!
He loves sharing and he thinks it is fun to care.
Big Bunny likes his food cut up
But at least he eats it.
I think Big Bunny is so very fluffy.
His fur is light brown with some white.
I love my pet and I hope you do too.

Mikayla Aimer (10)
St Mary's Hampton CE Primary School, Hampton

Gangster Cat

G angster Cat

A ctive star, brilliant cat.

N oisy cat roams through the night.

G enerous cat.

S ensible cat, goes through the daylight.

T ough cat, fights for truth and justice.

E ncourages others.

R un, the car is being chased!

C apable cat.

A bility to help others.

T rouble escaping.

Holly Griffin (10)

St Mary's Hampton CE Primary School, Hampton

The Ghost Of The Night

If you are lucky, you might be able to see,
The ghost of the night, high up in a tree.
As soon as it's midnight all the birds will follow,
The glowing ghost was queen in fact.
Above the clouds it was very packed.
But when the sun came up
The glowing stopped and birds flew down.
But the next night when the clock turns midnight
Look out for the glowing light.

Romilly Heywood (10)
St Mary's Hampton CE Primary School, Hampton

The Crazy Tortoise, McWheele

M ildly tame but kills cats all the time.

C ross and grumpy but most of all, super sickly.

W ild and stalks people.

H airy and can grow up to 10,000km.

E asy to tame or hard if it is 10,000km.

E vil and has a secret lair.

L ays over 100,000,000,000 eggs.

E asy to wash if you can catch it.

William Parish (8)

St Mary's Hampton CE Primary School, Hampton

Freddie The Fire Phoenix

F reddie is a fire phoenix and unsurprisingly hates water.

R eally alone, no son or daughter.

E very time he is always there,

D oing something with his fire hair.

D o you ever wonder if he is real?

I n the water he is friends with a seal.

E verybody loves Freddie the fire phoenix.

James Hannan (10)

St Mary's Hampton CE Primary School, Hampton

The Evil Blue Gangster Pigeon

P ing! Will you stop, argh! I'm trying to concentrate.

I give up! Just have my glasses... Hey, my headphones!

G reat! You're blue now and my paint, it costs lots.

E h, why are you in the paint, wait, OMG, get out!

O h you can rap, uh, wow!

N aughty bird, that's my radio.

Briar McKenna (10)
St Mary's Hampton CE Primary School, Hampton

Elasta Dog

E lastic.

L aser eyes.

A ny part of the body can extend.

S ad back story.

T ennis world champion.

A cid spit.

D eep down in the ocean he can still breathe.

O ne of a kind.

G reat Dane.

Dez Kordyl (9)

St Mary's Hampton CE Primary School, Hampton

The Colourful, Marvellous, Rainbow, Stretchy Bug

Late one night I was nearly asleep
A vibrant rainbow long bug flew into my brain
Then he jumped out of my brain.
We became best friends
He was rainbow
And was good at smelling and especially hearing.
A few days later he jumped back into my big brain.

Maddie Bissett (8)
St Mary's Hampton CE Primary School, Hampton

Bun Bun The Bunny

Bun Bun the bunny
Who is really, really funny.
Bun Bun the bunny
Lives in a jar of honey.
Bun Bun the bunny
Hates being in a cubby.
Bun Bun the bunny
Likes gummies with a jar of sweet honey.
Bun Bun the bunny
Loves being funny.

Vivienne Dzhikova (9)

St Mary's Hampton CE Primary School, Hampton

Drumo

D rums when he is bored.

R esponsible.

U ndercover as a talking K9.

M ostly reads books loudly, not that secretive.

O nly two people know, and that's my parents.

Drake Sequeira (10)

St Mary's Hampton CE Primary School, Hampton

Rufus The Acrobatic Spy

R eally good at acrobatics.

U ndercover spy.

F abulous trampoliner.

U sually is jumping around.

S earches for clues a lot.

Lauren Woods (10)

St Mary's Hampton CE Primary School, Hampton

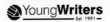

My Pet, Ridge

My pet is called Ridge,
His friend is a fridge.
He is a lion,
His coat is the colour cyan.
He really likes to sit,
For quite a bit.

Kareena Mahl (9)
St Mary's Hampton CE Primary School, Hampton

Daisy The Donkey

My donkey's name is Daisy
She likes to jump and bark.
She has back wings and hairy legs
But she really loves the park!

She doesn't eat donkey food
Because that puts her in a stinky mood.
The sound she makes in the middle of the night
Will definitely wake you in a fright.

She used to live in Donkey Land
But then she came to us
And told us that she planned to fly
All the way to the sky.

I love Daisy the donkey
Even though she's rough
I just can't wait to celebrate
Her big birthday when she's eight.

Rachel Wyllie (11)
The Glasgow Academy, Kelvinbridge

The Healing Cat

This furry, feeling feline
Loves cuddles and strokes
There's nothing that can stop her
Not even a sore throat.
She can fly through the clouds
And heal every hour
There is no one too ill
To be healed by her power.
She soothes with her magic touch
Her heart is pure and kind
Don't worry if you need her
She's not that hard to find.
Just close your eyes and count to ten
And make a special wish
And if you really want to please her
Leave out her favourite dish.

Milly Tabor Nunn (10)
The Glasgow Academy, Kelvinbridge

My Little Friend

You want to see a peculiar pet,
Well I bet you haven't seen mine yet!
It jumps from trees and swims in lakes.
You're thinking, *there must be some mistake?*
Well you see, she's just a little rainbow-coloured sheepy!
Her name is Clouds,
You're wondering why?
It's because she fell out from the sky!
I love her lots with all my heart,
Even though she does smell of rainbow farts!
Now, this is where my story ends,
It's always nice to think of our friends.

Laura Humphreys (10)
The Glasgow Academy, Kelvinbridge

My Tiny Pet

My tiny pet must be handled with care.
One strong gust will send him flying in the air!
My tiny pet looks young for his age
But being called 'cute' sends him into a rage!
My tiny pet loves a huge hug
Even though sometimes he just wants to sit on a cold rug.
My tiny pet had a huge day
So I'm just going to let him rest,
Night-night Johnny.

Lexi Mitchell (10)
The Glasgow Academy, Kelvinbridge

Colourful Koala

My colourful koala changes colours
It goes red when it's mad
And blue when it's sad,
Yellow when it's happy
And green when it's very snappy!
It shows all sorts of emotions,
It's like it's drunk loads of potions
But my koala can be cuddly and kind,
It might be small and fluffy
But it has a giant mind!

Erin Thomson (11)
The Glasgow Academy, Kelvinbridge

Carrot The Peculiar Parrot!

Carrot the parrot is a peculiar fellow,
When things don't go his way, he starts to bellow!

Carrot the parrot is on a diet,
I'll send you the ingredients, go on, try it!

Carrot the parrot loves to sleep,
But before he does, he cuddles up like a sheep!

Carrot the parrot has dozed off to sleep,
He sleeps in silence, not even a peep!

One thing about Carrot you need to know,
In the night, he starts to glow!

Eden Murray (12)
Townhill Primary School, Townhill

Super Sid

My pet Super Sid is a superhero dog
Sid has an Afro and he thinks he is a god
He was an orange sausage dog with a blue cape
Sid barked all of the time until he changed shape
Sid's favourite toy is a ball
And his favourite place to go is the waterfall
He swaggers when he walks
And he tumbles when he talks
His favourite food is steak
And Sid's owner likes to bake.

C Bosshardt (9)
Townhill Primary School, Townhill

YOUNG wRITERS INFORMATION

We hope you have enjoyed reading this book – and that you will continue to in the coming years.

If you're a young writer who enjoys reading and creative writing, or the parent of an enthusiastic poet or story writer, visit our website **www.youngwriters.co.uk/subscribe** to join the World of Young Writers and receive news, competitions, writing challenges, tips, articles and giveaways! There is lots to keep budding writers motivated to write!

If you would like to order further copies of this book, or any of our other titles, then please give us a call or order via your online account.

Young Writers
Remus House
Coltsfoot Drive
Peterborough
PE2 9BF
(01733) 890066
info@youngwriters.co.uk

**Join in the conversation!
Tips, news, giveaways and much more!**

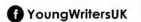 **YoungWritersUK** 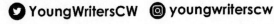 **YoungWritersCW**  **youngwriterscw**